Fifty Five

More Years

As remembered by Peter Harris

The Sequel to **The First Ten Years In Australia**

Max Barrington

Fifty Five More Years

Copyright © 2024 Max Barrington layout design and Copyright © 2024 by mph holding's Published in 2024 by Etteleah Books - Cairns Australia. cover and art by mph holding's

All rights reserved. No part of this book may be reproduced or transmitted in any form or by any means, electronic or mechanical, including photocopying, recording, or by information storage and retrieval system, without the author's permission

First published in Australia in 2024 by Etteleah Books - Cairns Australia
Fifty Five More Years ISBN:978-0975653883

Max Barrington

Fifty Five More Years

For the love of my life,
my darling wife and my inspiration,
Lynette

This book is based on a true story, names and places may have been changed

Max Barrington

Other Books by Max Barrington

Woolgar River Curse: Receiving a phone call announcing that you are the heir to a 70,000 acre cattle property that is complete with a five bedroom mansion would be like winning the Lotto. But to Gus and Lynette Teague, it was the beginning of a discovery into corruption, deceit, tragedy and murder. Was it really an 'Aboriginal Curse' on that property that caused the death of a family of five, or simply tragic events?

Task: I was looking to make a few dollars until my next work project started. "Check out the Air Tasking pages on Facebook," they said. An Australian road trip from Cairns to Darwin turns into Mystery, Intrigue and Life Threatening Danger

Dying to Find Gold:Fossicking for Gold in Australia is a popular activity. But when Mick West's, best mate goes missing whilst on a fossicking trip The police suspect Mick of murder.

The First Ten Years in Australia. From a 10 year old ten pound pom:
An Amazing story of a ten-year-old boy's adventure of coming from England to
Australia with his parents in 1959.
It tells of the family's ten moves to different New South Wales towns, within ten years, whilst his father sought work, from a ferry skipper to a quarry manager.
It, also tells of a determination, to succeed in a new environment.
A very moving, yet, such an interesting turn of events, of a real family, based on a true story.
You will not be able to put this book down!

The New March:
It was a hot day in the Far Northern Coastal Australian Town.
The first thing that Mitchell wanted as he walked into the sleepy town's public bar was a cool drink.
The last thing that Mitchell wanted, was to kill five people inside that sleepy town's public bar.

Bad Company:
Two people are arrested for murder in Far North Queensland, Australia in 2016 and refuse to reveal the location of the body.
Four years later an ex Police Officer discovers new evidence that could prove the convicted murderers to be innocent.

Max Barrington

Contents

Canberra	1
Townsville	12
Magnetic Island	21
Back to the Mainland	37
A Move to Cairns	54
A Big Move	71
Return to Townsville	85
Tablelands	97
Clockwise around Australia	113
Bundaberg	119
Back to Paradise	128

Max Barrington

Fifty Five More Years

Max Barrington

Canberra

It was 1989, thirty years since I had arrived at Pyrmont Docks Sydney with my parents, my brother and my sister from Blackpool in the United Kingdom in 1959. I can remember that day quite clearly and I recall it was October and that it was raining. I was ten years old.

The ship that we had arrived on was the S.S. Orontes. It was part of the Orient Line which became P&O Orient. Orontes was built in 1929 in England and it carried one thousand, six hundred passengers in two separate classes and had a crew of four hundred. The total number of persons on board was just two thousand and it travelled at a speed of around eighteen knots and had taken just on seven weeks to sail from Tilbury docks in England to Sydney Australia.

If you were to compare the Orontes, with a length of two hundred metres and a width of twenty two metres to, say the newest P&O Line ship, the Arvia, at a length of three hundred and forty four metres and a width of forty two metres and carrying a total of passengers and crew at almost seven thousand persons onboard. The Arvia cruises at a speed of twenty two knots, yes, that is only four more than the Orontes' eighteen knots, but on a ten thousand mile, or sixteen thousand kilometre journey, it means one whole week less travelling time.

We had spent some time living at a transitional hostel at East Hills, about thirty five kilometres south east of Sydney and after many moves, around ten, we settled in the Canberra suburb of Curtin where I completed an apprenticeship, conscripted and deferred for national service and became married.

If you have not yet done so you might like to read my previous book that covers this period, *The First Ten Years in Australia'*.

I had many diversified types of employment following my apprenticeship including operating earth moving machinery, driving a concrete agitator and driving tourist coaches. Some people would refer to my employment during that period between 1972 and 1982 as *'more starts than Pharlap'*.

I had also become separated and divorced from my wife during that time and had later become remarried.

Somewhere between the ages of about twenty three and thirty three, when I look back, seem to be the dark stages of my life, through my own doing I admit.

For some reason, I believe I was a complete fool during this period and I have no answer why.

I can't say that 'I fell in with the wrong crowd', although that would be much easier, nor can I really say that I was misled, because quite often, I was alone.

I did at one stage have a mate who was German by birth. Paul was his name, he was an auto electrician who had a business just around the corner from my business in Fyshwick, as a locksmith, and we were both keen shooters.

He would call around, unannounced, to my place in his FJ50 short wheelbase Landcruiser, at any time of the week, or day, complete with a full esky of beer, a whole rump some sausages and his rifles and say 'Mein Freund, komm wir gehen jagen' (my friend, come we are going hunting). I would say to him to give me a minute to finish whatever it was I was doing and tell my staff that I would be back later, then jump in the cruiser with him and call around to my home to collect some clothing and my rifle and shotgun and we would be gone for anywhere to a week. Just stupidity.

    I had another friend. Lloyd, who was also a Locksmith. He had a contract with one of the major Australian banks to service their 'safe locks' and other 'locks' at their country branches throughout New South Wales, he also had a pilot's license and hired a Cessna 124 aircraft from the Canberra Areo Club to fly to the various bank locations.

On occasions, when he required assistance at a branch, I would fly with him to various outback New South Wales towns. I remember on one such trip, the weather turned rough while we were working at a bank at Beckom, some three hundred and fifty kilometres from Canberra and we were unable to fly back that night.

We had such a big night of trying to drink the pub dry together with a contingent of shearers that the next morning Lloyd was in no condition to fly the plane back to Canberra until two days later.

These are just two of many examples that I can recall but really don't wish to repeat them here.

I always seemed to be the last one to leave a party.

If I happened to be in a pub at closing time I would find a club that was still open.

Some people would jokingly call me 'The Moth' as I would go wherever there was a light.

An interesting note on my old German friend Paul.

Paul was also married at the time that we would recklessly go off camping and shooting with little regard towards our families. His wife's name was Ricky and they had one child back in those days, around the mid to late 1970's.

It was, I think in 2007, Joy and I were visiting my mother at her home in Redcliffe, Queensland.

It was a dreary, rainy sort of a day and my mother gave me a paperback book to read.

The book was called 'Almost Perfect Murder'.

As I started to read the book, I had a strange sensation or feeling come over me which I can't really explain and then I suddenly realised that the book I was reading, about a murdered woman in the Australian Capital Territory, that woman was Paul's wife or, ex wife.

It was a very eerie feeling and little pieces started to come together as I continued to read to confirm that it was indeed Paul's ex wife.

But I did finally come back to earth.

I had returned to my trade with the Department of Housing and Construction and became a works supervisor where I worked my way to a senior technical officer. During this period I attended college and attained a degree in applied science. This allowed me to become head of my section within the department.

I learned very early in this department to watch my back, insomuch as jealous fellow office staff. I discovered that many people were in fact 'smiling assassins' who would sink you before cover for you.

It seemed to me that their sole purpose of attending the office each day was to see how many rungs up the ladder they could achieve regardless of whom they sank or retarded that day.

I also learned never to refuse any courses that were available to me through the department. One that I nearly passed on was computing, simply because back then it was a totally 'new thing'. I had originally enrolled on a simple word processing course but after only one day in the class, I was sent to attend a typing class as I was slowing down the word processing class.

It worked out well, as by the time I had completed the typing class and had attained the mandatory minimum amount of words per minute, the word processing course was finished so I took on a database and spreadsheet course instead which really got me interested in computing to the extent that I followed on with programming courses.

It was in 1988 that I bumped into an old Lyneham High School friend that was living in Brisbane
But was back in Canberra to attend a funeral. I had not seen David in many years and we had a great get-together and attempted to 'drink dry' the Ainslie Rex Hotel's public bar, 'the dugout'.

We had exchanged phone numbers and addresses (mobile telephones were not invented) and we vowed to keep in touch, which we did and David contacted me in May 1988 to advise me that through his work he had been given passes to 'Expo 88' that was being held in Brisbane and suggested that my wife and I stay with them in Brisbane and attend the expo.

In my twenty nine years of living in Australia, not once had I been to Queensland. I had travelled extensively in New South Wales and Victoria, but never had I stepped foot into Queensland.

We had organised flights for early flights from Canberra to Brisbane and it was on a very cold, frosty and then later foggy, June morning that we sat at the Canberra airport waiting for our fog delayed flight to depart, the temperature that morning was minus four degrees celsius.

We didn't arrive at Brisbane until just after midday and sadly my friend David who was picking us up from the airport was not there to collect us as he could not wait any longer and had to return to his work, which we had assumed after some time looking for him.

It was twenty three degrees as we waited at the airport bus stop and it was just great, I was starting to wonder why I was living in the Australian Capital Territory.

Expo 88 was just fantastic, sadly we only had a one day pass and it would easily take a full week to see all of the expo. There were queues everywhere to see the exhibits and the first queue that we got into, we thought, was for Queensland forestry products turned out to be a queue for baby pusher hire. It wasn't until later, when having lunch, that we should have realised that all the people in the queue were carrying children, we enjoyed a laugh. What a great day we had at Expo 88.

Following the day at the Expo, David had taken the day off work and we ventured down to the Gold Coast and Jupiters Casino. This was a first for me, I had never been to a casino before and I was amazed, not just at the gambling part but also the restaurants and the food at such affordable prices, Canberra had nothing like this. During the short, three day, stay in Brisbane, I had fallen in love with the climate and the activity of Brisbane.

Returning to a wet, cold and foggy day in Canberra, it was back to work the next day with very fond memories of the last few days in Brisbane I had instantly decided that I wanted to move from Canberra to Brisbane and firstly discussed it with my wife who wasn't too sure she could handle the heat in Brisbane but thought that the city itself was great and that a move might be good, and agreed to give it a try.

I had not been back at work for ten minutes when I found the human resources officer at our complex and enquired about a transfer to Brisbane.

He asked me if I could make my own way to Yass as that's where the queue starts (Yass is a small rural village about sixty kilometres from Canberra). In other words, there were that many people in our department who wanted to transfer to Brisbane, unbelievable.

The following weekend I bought The Brisbane 'Courier Mail' newspaper and scoured the 'position's vacant' but of course, I could find nothing that could compare to the position that I had with the department in both work description and remuneration, so, that seemed to be the end of that exercise and I decided to get on with life in the A.C.T.

That weekend the weather was miserable, it was too cold to go into the garden, or to go anywhere for that matter. Hmmmm Brisbane, I checked the newspaper that I had bought for the Brisbane weather report, No! It was twenty four there today and sunny, it's not fair and I decided that I would keep on getting the Courier Mail newspaper each Saturday and look for some acceptable positions in Brisbane.

I seemed to be 'obsessed' with moving to Brisbane, I had lost interest in my superb job that I had and my beautiful home at Isabella Plains in the A.C.T. I wanted to move to a warmer climate. I was fed up with the cold Canberra winters. People say that it can't be that bad, well it 'fucking is' that bad and now when I look back I really don't know how I put up with it.

I know it's me, I know that lots of people love Canberra and especially it's winters! But I also know that a lot of people don't and I am now one of them.

If you have never lived there then you can't appreciate waking up in the winter time mornings and staying in the shower until the hot water goes cold and you *have* to get out, get dressed and try to stay warm after the hot shower.

You have to go out in the freezing cold and start your car to get it warm and if you don't have a carport or garage then you have to get the ice off the windscreen.

The same would be true if you went out at night somewhere for dinner, ice would form on the windscreen of your car, and when you left the restaurant, you had to sit in your freezing car waiting for the ice to melt, sorry but! Fuck that, I am just so glad that they are but memories these days.

Reflecting on Canberra, I arrived at Sutton New South Wales, which is just north of the Australian Capital Territory border, with my family in 1962 at the age of thirteen and attended Lyneham High School. Getting to school each day was quite an experience, being driven by car to the New South Wales border where the bus would collect us for the journey into various Canberra suburbs.

1965 saw the family move from Sutton to the Canberra suburb of Curtin. Now in 1988 after twenty six years of Living in the area, I was seriously contemplating moving to Queensland, it would be a big move for me.

I think the saddest thing about leaving was my two sons but I would return from time to time and I would certainly keep in touch with them, which I still do today, and my job which I absolutely loved, I think that I had been very lucky to secure the position and the position offered me so many challenging projects and advanced educational opportunities. Of course, I would also miss my parents and friends.

Despite my regular Saturday perusing of the Courier Mail, it wasn't until late 1989 that I found what I thought might be a suitable position, not in Brisbane but Townsville, the position advertised was for a project manager on small to medium construction projects in North Queensland.

My application for the position attracted an interview in Brisbane and the company organised air travel and accommodation. I returned to Canberra with the job and submitted my resignation to the department the following day.

I was bombarded with counter offers to stay with the department in the form of working fewer hours, an upgrade to my government, home garaged, car in the form of private number plates to allow for the private use of the vehicle. I was offered all sorts of little perks but no extra pay as my position was at its remuneration limit. I had sadly declined all offers as my eyes were firmly fixed on moving to Queensland and even the stories that I was told about how wild, remote and hot Townsville was, would not deter me and the house was put on the market and it was a Thursday morning about two weeks before Christmas 1989 that I, together with my wife and our two cattle dogs, Max & Sandy, boarded an aeroplane for Sydney, Brisbane and finally Townsville.

The company that I was now employed by had organised and paid for the removal of our furniture in Canberra to a storage facility in Townsville. Farewell Canberra.

Townsville

I was met at the Townsville airport by the company's construction manager, Bob, who welcomed both my wife and myself to Townsville, he had organised a boarding kennel to collect and house our two cattle dogs for as long as required, and he had given me the keys to a brand new Holden Commodore sedan that was parked at the airport along with directions to the hotel accommodation that was to be provided by the company until we had found a house to either rent or buy with the emphasis on 'take your time, no rush'.

'Bob also made a mutually agreed time to meet with us the next morning for a tour of Townsville and the company offices followed by lunch at the Townsville Casino. What with all this and... a beautiful thirty degrees, although cloudy, temperature, I was of the opinion that things just couldn't get better.

The Saturday morning following the tour of Townsville, which had included the location of the boarding kennels at a place called 'the Bohle', we had visited our dogs at the kennels and the kennel owner suggested that we take them for a run at 'Bushland Beach' a small beach community just north of the Bohle, where he said, there were extensive grassed areas for them to run.

I didn't really like putting the dogs into the brand new commodore and we hadn't even thought that we would be taking them for a drive in the car, but thought that it would not hurt.

We arrived at Bushland Beach, wow! What a great spot with very few houses that were away from the beach leaving a large grassed area in front of the beach.

I let the dogs out of the car and in a flash they were on the beach and into the water swimming, 'Oh no!' We had no towels or anything to try to dry them or attempt to remove the wet sand with so we sat on the grassed area with the dogs on a lead for about an hour hoping that they would dry off. You can imagine the mess on the back seat of the commodore after we had dropped the dogs back at the kennel.

The first Sunday in Townsville and it was pissing down with rain, we went to the Castletown Shopping Centre, mainly just for a look around and to get minor items like toothpaste and such. I parked the car in the basement to avoid getting wet and we enjoyed wandering around the centre for about an hour.

We had noticed that there seemed to be roof leaks in the centre as wheelie bins were being placed in areas to collect the water, we could also hear the roar of the rain on the roof of the shopping centre, but we failed to instantly hear the warnings to owners of cars that were parked in the basement, by the time we did it was almost too late.

We walked almost knee deep in water to the new commodore that had water just past the bottom of the doors, opening the doors to get into the car allowed water to flood the carpeted floor of the commodore and we drove back to the hotel in the pouring rain with water sploshing around the floor and causing all the windows to fog up and I could not see a thing, 'Fuck' what a mess my brand new, one hundred and nine kilometres on the clock, company car was, the back seats were covered in mud and sand from the dogs and now the floors were flooded in water and I hadn't even started work for the company yet.

Apparently, we were lucky as many cars were completely flooded in that car park on that day, the army was called in and towed many cars from the basement park using Unimog vehicles.

My first day at my new job found me using a wet vacuum cleaner, fortunately, that the company had, to remove the water from my car. The company GM told me to be careful around the area as it was very prone to flooding during the wet season and the drowning of vehicles was fairly common at this time.

Following that I was introduced to some of the office staff and was put with another project manager, Ian, to assist him and learn the ropes until I was handed a project.

This construction company, although competitive in all types of commercial development, specialised on medium-density units and had a system where, depending on the size of the project, the project manager did the initial quantity surveying and cost estimating the the entire project and once the construction was approved would then be responsible for its construction.

Quantity Surveying, was not new to me as I had completed a basic, accredited, course for this with the department, but I was astounded by how Ian manually calculated his measurements into quantities as his desktop computer sat idle.

'Don't you use your PC for quantities?' I asked him.

'What do you mean, how can my computer generate estimates' Ian replied.

He then told me that they only use computers for databases, that is for project cost recording.

He had not heard of a computer program called Lotus123, when I told him of it's function as a spreadsheet and how it was used by the department in project construction he became very interested.

As it turned out, the Lotus123 program had been installed on all the PCs in the office but it seems that no one had any idea of what it does.

I quickly gave Ian a demonstration by putting together a few simple macros on a spreadsheet that would calculate construction material quantities from just a few measurements. Ian was blown away and immediately called the general manager and asked him to come to look at what I had put on his PC. The general manager was also most impressed with my simple spreadsheet and simple macro display which I had set up in a matter of minutes.

'That is nothing' I boasted, unbelieving that they had no knowledge of this program. 'I can set up a spreadsheet that will not only give you most of the construction material quantities required for the entire project from basic measurements but also the individual costings'

The general manager just glared at me in amazement.

The department in which I worked in Canberra was very focused on the employment and implementation of personal computers, although still in its infancy in many ways, information technology experts were employed under contract to asses manual methods that were engaged in day to day procedures and specify, or create a suitable program for various tasks. Staff were then trained in computing and software applications.

I had attended many certified courses for various programs and their applications including programming with Turbo Pascal, that were provided by the department.

I had made mention of my computing skills in my resume to the construction company but it seemed that they had not really considered it as they were, it would seem, to be virtually computer illiterate in other than database, payroll and word processing. Maybe Queensland was behind? I had been told by my former workmates that it was solely run by banana benders.

Things were progressing well with work once I had been taught about the mysteries (to Me) of besser block construction which is a widespread system of construction in north and far north Queensland.

In my first few days whilst working with Ian on his new project I had allowed for a quantity of UA Steel Sections for lintel spans.

'What are these for Peter?' Asked Ian referring to the steel sections.

'Mainly window and sliding door openings' I replied matter of factually, wondering why he would ask.

'But we have bond beams at those locations' he said.

'Bond beams? What are bond beams?' I asked, genuinely confused.

I then told Ian that I had never worked with concrete masonry block construction before, in fact, I had never even seen it before as most construction around Canberra was brick, composite or concrete panel.

Ian then produced a Besser block catalogue that displayed the many types of blocks produced such as 'bond beam blocks' which are designed with only side walls and base, there is no top or rib, this is to allow reinforcing steel to pass through a course of blocks which is then filled with concrete to form a beam, hence the word 'bond beam'. There are also many other types of blocks for different constructional functions.

It didn't stop there, I then had to learn about 'cyclone rating construction' that starts with tie-downs in the concrete footings or slabs and continues to the tie-down point of the truss chords. I won't go on and bore you here with construction details, as much as I love construction and methodology, this is not a technical book.

We had been looking around at homes to buy as after a month of living in a hotel was getting us down.
Bob, the GM at work knew a real estate agent and the agent had made contact with us and had offered to show us a few properties. The first property that he showed us was a tidy little home on a small acreage, it looked quite impressive and we assumed it would be well out of our price range.
We had sold our home in Isabella Plains at a very good price of around one hundred and eighty thousand dollars and our home buying budget for Townsville was around the same price, this home looked to us, to be well over that amount. We were shocked to hear the asking price of this tidy acreage home was 'seventy five' thousand, we both thought that we had missed the 'one hundred and' part.

We had been in Townsville for just on four months and were enjoying living in our new home on acreage, our dogs were the happiest with their new lifestyle of having acres to run around on rather than the seven hundred square metre property in Canberra.

It was on this fourth month, April, April the fourth to be exact that category three Cyclone Aivu crossed the coast near Home Hill, about halfway between Townsville and Bowen causing over ninety million dollars in damage. That was a lot of money in 1989.

It had been our first cyclone and we were terrified as our neighbours had told us that a cat three cyclone could be quite dangerous but that it would most likely 'fizz out' before it made landfall.

The telephone book was the source of information with respect to cyclones back then and we followed all the instructions to a tee, much to the amusement of our neighbours who considered that we had gone overboard with the cyclone preparations and told us that we would get used to them as they were fairly frequent visitors to Townsville.

As it turned out it was just a bit of a blow but the amount of rain was unbelievable and it was impossible for me to get to work for nearly a week.

The road system to me around Townsville seemed ridiculous with roads going downhill towards creeks and rivers with a small bridge to cross, these all flooded and closed the roads until well after heavy rainfalls. The local mentality was that it's only in the wet season that they flood and they seemed to just get on with it, 'just a bit inconvenient for a couple of months' they said.

I had only been with my new job in Townsville for about six months when the whispers started that the company I worked for was going down.

I asked Ian my colleague at work if this rumour was true and he suggested that it was just that, a rumour, and it was most likely started by one of our opposition companies. Later that day when I went to leave I could not get access to the basement car park, I went and saw the general manager and he told me that unfortunately the building where the office was located, although owned by the construction company had been repossessed by the companies financier and the basement had been closed and the other two floors would follow and that the company would be shutting down until a new financier was found.

I was then asked for my car keys and was told that I could get a cheque later that day for money I was owed in wages. Well, not off to a good start.

Magnetic Island

Before this shock with my workplace, we had decided to sell our property and buy a house on Magnetic Island that had caught our eye. It was on Picnic Street next to the mall at Picnic Bay. My wife had accepted a job with the Magnetic Island Ferry as its hostess and she could start and finish her shift on the island and I could easily commute to Townsville for my work each day.

Now I was laid off from my work we decided to go ahead and move over to the island where I would seek some other sort of work.

As luck would have it, I was lucky to score a job driving a tourist bus on the island, the money was very poor at about one quarter of what I was being paid by the construction company but the job was nothing short of a fun filled day of taking tourists around the island and lunching at the Lattitude 19 resort where I received a free lunch every day in exchange for taking the tourists there. This job was only a four hour a day shift for four days a week, which left me plenty of time. We had bought a sailboat, a twenty nine foot Vancouver cutter rigged sloop that had sailed from Vancouver in Canada to Townsville, the yacht's name was 'Kaila'.

I worked weekends on a charter boat that did fishing trips that left Townsville on Friday night and returned on Sunday lunchtime and this was very good money but better still, it was a great experience to learn about the local reefs and fishing spots.

I applied to the port authority for a Smooth Waters Coxwains License and was given a logbook and told that I must log at least one hundred and fifty hours working on a commercial vessel over a minimum of twenty days and I had to pass an open book test using the publication 'Small Ships Manual'.

Doug, the owner of the Reef Link Ferry Service, whom my wife worked for, gave me days on the ferry 'Reeflink One' to help fill my logged time.

The engineer on board Reeflink also owned the scooter hire that was based in the Picnic Bay mall and he asked me if I could run it for him each Monday, which was also another form of income.

Sadly all my island jobs were casual and seasonal with most businesses on the island shutting down from December to Easter each year back in those days as tourism was pretty quiet during the wet season period.

There were, however, plenty of German and other nationalities, backpackers around Townsville and Magnetic Island during the wet season and I started a very lucrative business taking these backpackers from Townsville for a sail around Magnetic Island at fifty dollars a head, lunch included, which I provided by getting cooked chooks from woolies each morning as I arrived in Townsville from Maggie to collect the passengers, these I cut into fours together and with some tomatoes, lettuce and cucumber make an excellent and easy smorgasbord lunch, followed by some watermelon and cantaloupe, I took up to six passengers at a time and the lunch cost me less than thirty dollars each day. I allowed the passengers to bring along their favourite drinks, which they would invariably leave some of them each day for me to collect and of course, consume with my onboard lunch while they swam at Radical Bay on a scheduled stop. Magic! And good money.

It was a Monday in May 1992, and I was working at the scooter hire when thirteen American sailors from the visiting submarine the US Chicago arrived wanting to hire scooters, there were only twelve hire scooters in the fleet which I hired to them but I was one scooter short.
The guy who owned the scooters lived on the mainland and I tried to call him at his home to ask if I could hire out his own personal scooter which he kept at the hire shop. I couldn't get him so I thought 'What the hell' and I hired out his almost new Honda Scoopy scooter to the last sailor.

The sailors had hired the scooters for the full day and had returned in dribs and drabs that afternoon with the last back before five o'clock. Some of the scooters had suffered damage and the guys were happy to pay for it without any hassles and I went with them to the pub next door and had a few beers.
They were all, but one, Cheif Petty Officers, they told me that was the minimum rank aboard the Chicago and one of

them called Andy, who was a lieutenant invited myself and my wife for dinner on board the Chicago the next evening, I was honoured and said that we would be there and one of then issued me with his full name and rank to give to the security at the gate at the Townsville dock.

We sailed our boat 'Kaila' over to Townsville the next evening and tied up at our finger on the Townsville Charter Boat Marina so we would have accommodation for the night after dinner as the ferries stop running at ten pm and we walked the two point seven kilometres to the security gates at the Townsville Port and told the security officer that we had an appointment with Lt. Bingham 4927 at berth nine, the security officer made a phone call and then said to wait here and he will come over.

We waited for about three minutes when a splendidly dressed CPO walked up to us, I didn't recognise him in his uniform and he told me he was Barry and then said this way please Peter.

The was an armed sailor at the gangplank to the submarine at both the shore end and the submarine end. Aboard the Los Angeles-class submarine the USS Chicago (SSN-721) we were first given a tour of the vessel and learned that it had a complement of twelve officers and ninety eight men. The Chicago only had forty bunks as it was described as a 'hot bunking' vessel which meant that each bunk was shared by three men, who in turn had the bunk for only eight hours each day.

Due to the 'hot bunking' situation, over seventy of Chicago's crew were in hotel accommodation whilst the submarine was in dock. We were shown the officer's mess which looked pretty flashy and we met up with Andy, who also looked different in his uniform.

USS Chicago hats were given to us before we dined on, what they called 'ribbon steak' and vegetables followed by cake and ice cream made on board with their ice cream machine. I remembered one of the chefs from the scooter hire. A good evening.

We had both the charter boat mariner berth in Ross Creek and also a mooring at Picnic Bay, our boat Kaila, could be seen on the mooring from our house on Picnic Street through the kitchen window which looked towards the jetty. We also kept our dingy on the beach beside the house and the small outboard motor for it in the downstairs, under the high set house, laundry.

Generally, when I was in the kitchen I would look across at Kaila, one morning I looked across and didn't see Kaila. It was weird, I distinctly remember. I looked again and I could not see Kaila. I went down to the beach, that's about fifty metres from the house, Kaila was not on the mooring. I didn't know what to do, I just kept looking. Then it became reality, all of a sudden, Kaila was gone. I ran up toward the Picnic Bay jetty thinking that if she had broken free of the mooring she might be on the other side of the jetty which I could not see from the house. I knew well before reaching the jetty that she was not there. Where to look?

I ran back along the beach with my eyes scouring the bay to the house and into the laundry to get the small outboard motor, back to the beach where the dingy lay upside down on the sand.

Once in the dingy, I motored past the jetty and along the coastline toward West Point and I saw a boat outline that was almost on the shore, it was Kaila.

She was sitting with the bow slightly raised on a mudbank close to the shore, the mooring line lay limp over the bow roller and down to the water where it floated. I motored up to the stern and tied off the dingy and climbed on board going to the bow and pulling in the mooring line and coiling it on the deck as it came up. The end came up and the 'D' shackle, minus the pin, could be seen in the eye splice at the end of the mooring line. The pin had dislodged from the shackle somehow.

I went to the cockpit and then down below to the engine room and started the motor, back up into the cockpit and pushed the control for reverse and applied a little throttle, nothing happened. I applied more throttle and Kaila shuddered but remained fast in the mud and the tide was running out.

My mind was racing, the only other person that I knew with a boat big enough to pull Kaila free was Laurie at West Point but I thought that by the time I got back to the house and got my utility to drive to West Point it would be too late and the tide would be out and Kaila laying on her side.

Something made me remember that I had an old snatch strap that I used in my old Landcruiser FJ 40 that I had put onboard Kaila 'as it might come in handy one day' and this was the day!

I had tied the snatch strap to a piece of rope that I tied between the aft bollards of Kaila and the other end on a piece of rope that I had tied to both of the welded stern handles on the dingy.

I was now in the dingy with about five metres of slack snatch strap floating in the water and gave the throttle of the outboard full bore. The dingy shot forward and reaching the end of the slack, came to a sudden halt that threw me all the way to the bow and almost overboard, I had hit my knee on the centre seat of the dingy and there was blood everywhere. But, Kaila was off the mud and freely floating. I do not know how I did it but I remember going very shaky.

I now had no mooring so I took Kaila back to Picnic Bay and anchored in the bay just off from the beach and took the dingy back to shore. I couldn't leave Kaila on anchor in the bay indefinitely and I organised my friend Laurie at West Point, who is a diver, to reinstate the mooring. After Laurie's first dive on the mooring, he had come up laughing telling me that the mooring base was an old V8 motor block just sitting in the mud.

Laurie, installed a new line and 'D' shackle and also wired, with stainless steel wire, the pin of the shackle to prevent any turning of the pin.

Laurie would not accept any payment for fixing the mooring but asked if I could help him.

Laurie lived at West Point in a beach house that he had built with the intention of establishing a backpackers resort. He was now enjoying a reasonable occupancy and would collect his guests from the Picnic Bay ferry terminal in an open long wheel base Landrover troop carrier, type of vehicle. There was no electricity at West Point and the road to West Point was four wheel drive only. There were, at that stage no other dwellings other than some fishing shacks. Laurie's lodge was almost on the beach and it was common knowledge that the sand flies stopped many visitors from returning.

The police random breath testing unit would visit Magnetic Island by way of the vehicular ferry from time to time. The Island residents would be alerted of this via the 27meg radio on the barge to the Picnic Bay hotel, so it was generally just tourists that were at risk of being breathalysed. Laurie, obviously, hadn't received the warning on the day that the breath test unit pulled him over in his Landrover at Picnic Bay and he lost his driver's license for eight months.

Laurie now asked me if I could do his ferry transfers for him until he got his license back.

What could I say? Yes of course, and he also offered to pay me. He said that he would set the transfer times to meet the ferry at eight o'clock in the mornings and at five o'clock in the evenings.

I could make that work, especially for Laurie whom I had a lot of respect and time for.

When the prawns were running, after I dropped off his five o'clock evening transfers, Laurie and myself would go prawning on the beach in front of his house with his drag net and generally get around ten kilos in a few hours. Laurie had a wood fuelled copper and would cook the prawns in seawater that night and I would collect them the next morning when I arrived with his transfer. I would take the prawns home and buy around six bags of ice, weigh out the prawns in half-kilo lots, put them into medium size freezer bags, put them on ice in my two eskies and sell them to the Picnic Bay hotel where I would be paid for the prawns and go halves with Laurie.

I can tell you that the money that we received from the sale of the prawns would hardly cover the cost of the amount of beer that we drank when catching them. It was all good fun and easy work as the backpackers would often do all the work, we just drank beer while we watched and stoked the fire under the copper.

After the transfers for Laurie, I would head over to Townsville if I had any charters, I had organised to do charters only on Tuesdays, Fridays and Sundays and only when the weather permitted.

I remember one Tuesday when the four people didn't turn up at the marina and I had already bought the chicken, salad and fruit. So I called the 'Reeflink' ferry that my wife worked on, by 27meg radio and left a message with the skipper, whom I knew quite well, that I would pick her up in the dingy and bring her back to Kaila for lunch.

We enjoyed lunching on chicken and salads and I returned her back to the ferry in the dingy. Having got back to the marina, I undid the outboard motor clamps to put the motor away in a locker on board Kaila. I was kneeling on the back seat of the dingy, the clamps were undone and I did, as always, lift off the motor and slide it onto the marina pontoon. As I let go of the motor on the pontoon, for some strange reason, unbelievably, the motor slipped off the pontoon and into the water.

I don't know how it had slid off the pontoon, I quickly got my diving mask from Kaila and dived in to retrieve my outboard motor. It was about three meters down and standing up straight as the prop had gone into the mud, I grabbed the front carry handle and pulled as I kicked furiously in the water with my feet. It had seemed like a lifetime to get to the surface and I thought that I would not make it as the weight of the motor was winning, but I finally got to the surface and I had hold of the outboard in my right hand and I reached up to the pontoon and got a grip on a bollard.

I was in the water hanging onto the bollard with one hand while my other hand gripped the motor but I couldn't do anything. I could not lift the outboard up with my right hand, it was just too heavy, and if I let go of the pontoon with my left hand I would sink, 'Help' I screamed.

There were generally people walking around the pontoon going and coming from their boats, 'Help...help' I called but there was no one there.

I had no option and I let go of the outboard and let it once again sink to the bottom. I got onto the pontoon and grabbed a length of light rope from Kaila and dived back in where the outboard had sank.

The motor was lying on its side this time and a little more difficult to stand up and I had to resurface for air, then down again, and this time I managed to get the rope through the handle of the outboard motor and swam back to the surface with both ends of the rope.

Back on the pontoon with the rope and I started to pull up on both ends of the rope and now there were other people on the pontoon and I had help to pull it up.

I tied the outboard to the mast in an upright position and took off its cover and let it dry. After about an hour I removed the spark plug and gently pulled on the starting cord a few times, then with the spark plug replaced I gave it a good pull and it started the first time and it was as good as new again.

It was something that a lot of the island's residents would say to me from time to time.

'Be careful not to catch 'Island Fever'. I asked what is 'Island Fever' and I was told that it would just get me and I would not realise it until it was too late. They told me that my friend Laurie from West Point had it and to look at him carefully and I would see what it was.

'Island Fever' on Magnetic Island, according to some locals, was to let one's self go as it were, to give up on work, or not to take it seriously as if to say that you didn't have to work once you had enough money for the day.
Another sign of the fever was to start having a beer for breakfast.
I took a good look at myself and I could really see that *was* happening to me.

Often when I arrived at Lauries house on the morning transfer run I would have a beer, sometimes two or even three beers with Laurie and we would eat some of the prawns that we had caught the previous night.
More than once Laurie had offered me more beer as I was about to leave for the hotel with the prawns for sale and I had said,

'Yeah, why not? Fuck it, life can wait for a while'. and that was not good, and now I could see this was happening to me and, suddenly, I knew that I had to get out of this, get back to reality, get a job, get a purpose. Which I did.

I had told Laurie that I could not do his transfers any longer, that was not an easy task but he would be getting his license back within about a month anyway.

I started looking for a job that was off the island, as I knew that to work on the island I would fall back into my old routine and I did not want that to happen.

I had caught the ferry over to Townsville to attend an employment interview with a ceramic tile company as a sales rep. Not ideal, but Hey. Following the appointment, I had a wait of over an hour for the next ferry and went into Tattersalls Hotel in Flinders Street for lunch and had a chance to meet with Dale who ran an internal lining company.

I had met Dale while working at my previous job with the construction company, Dale was one of the company's favoured sub-contractors.

As fate would have it, Dale was looking for an estimator and asked if I could start with him on the following Monday. Why not?

Dale had met me, as arranged, at the Townsville ferry terminal the following Monday morning and had taken me to his office, he had shown me to an old FJ Landcruiser long wheelbase ute and had told me to use as required for the job and to park it at the ferry terminal each afternoon after work, sounded good to me.

I had some experience with partitioning and ceilings and had no problems knocking out estimates for new work projects for Dale's company, in fact, I quite enjoyed it as much of his work required site visits which meant that I was not stuck in the office and he paid me quite well.

I was commuting back to the island each day and all was good with the exception that Aborigine people seemed to enjoy sleeping in the back of the FJ cruiser each night and sometimes would still be in the back asleep when I arrived at the ferry terminal to collect the ute, or sometimes there was just their bedding, if you could call it that, left in the tray back which I would have to pick up and throw on to the ground, it stunk.

Other times there would be piles of empty beer cans and bottles, wine casks, food wrappers, takeaway meal remains and all sorts of shit that the brothers had left in the back of my ute. Fucking animals.

After about a year of working with Dale, I had been told by one of his tradies that a new internal linings manufacturing company that was just starting up in Australia was looking for a local rep in Townsville, he had kept the number for reply and gave it to me.

I did not hesitate and contacted the number and was advised that interviews for the position were being held the following week in Townsville and I was given the address to forward a resume together with an expression of interest, which I had completed and forwarded.

It was some days later, on one afternoon after returning to the island, that I had found a phone message on the home phone answering unit at my home in Picnic Bay, my only contact number as mobile telephones were in their infancy at that time.

I returned the call to the mobile number that was quoted in the message that same afternoon and spoke to Allen who advised me that he would be conducting interviews at the Townsville Casino, where he would be staying next week, and he asked if I could attend.

At the interview with Allen, he advised that he was the state sales manager with the recently formed building products branch of a well known and recognised national Australian company, that had also recently acquired a national Besser block manufacturer and distributor. He went on to say that currently there are only two major manufacturers of the internal lining product in Australia and that his company was presently conducting research and viability studies in various locations and would welcome me on board as the area manager for Far North Queensland, but my territory would initially include Hervey Bay, Rockhampton, Townsville and Cairns with, of course, every town in between.

I was told of the excellent remuneration package which also included a company car, which was a Holden Commodore, and membership to the Ansett Golden Wing Club. The latter had me wondering why, but the answer came soon enough.

I accepted the position graciously but inside I felt that I had just won the lottery, Wow!

The first part of my job was to be product knowledge training that would take part in Sydney, New South Wales. Back to the cold, I thought!

I would leave Townsville each Monday on the first flight to Sydney and would return each Friday on the first flight out of Sydney and I would attend training at the Sydney manufacturing facility each Tuesday, Wednesday and Thursday.

Accommodation and all meals of course were provided together with transport from the hotel to the facility.

The hotel I stayed at was the Coogee Bay Boutique Hotel, five star accommodation with food to match, I lived like a king.

The big problem was of course leaving my wife on her own on the island, she was safe, and that was not the issue, the problem was that I would have to go to Townsville on the Sunday night in order to catch the flight on Monday morning as the ferry service morning arrival in Townsville would miss the flight and it was touch and go with the returning flights on the Fridays to catch the last ferry to the island, which meant that I had to be away from our home in Picnic Bay for six nights of the week! But it would only be for about three months. We'll see how we go.

Back to the Mainland

We didn't go too well and decided to find a house somewhere around Townsville and sell our beautiful home at Picnic Bay. This in itself was very difficult because I was never home during the week. My wife organised everything, the sale of the island property and the purchase of a new home at Pallaraenda a beachside suburb.

I took one week off from my work to help with the moving and life went much easier following the move. I didn't have to leave home now until Monday morning and I was back home on Friday night which meant that I was only away for four nights each week, believe me, it made a big difference.

There were seven of us, from different parts of Australia, doing the course in Sydney, there were two other area managers and four sales representatives.

This company used a uniform word processing, spreadsheet and database in all of its operations that allowed it to combine into one large reporting system for the whole entity.

The Internet had not yet been invented.

It was unbelievable that the systems employed by this company were very similar to those of the department and were operated in a very similar way, these programs were somewhat advanced from the department's systems but nether the less, the same. Needless to say, I blitzed the Class on the computing course.

The training covered the aspect of the lining operation that was to be a franchise distribution system.

The area manager's role was to establish a distribution centre at various, strategic, locations within their territories, stock them and then employ and train suitable staff to turn them into a working distribution centre and then find a suitable franchisee to purchase and run the internal lining's distribution.

Unbeknown to me, whilst in Sydney attending my training, the newly acquired Besser side of the company had decided to get into the lining side of the business also. The area manager for the Besser manufacturing, Armin, who covered the same area that my new territory would cover, being an opportunist, had put it to the head office that his existing block plants become the internal lining distribution points. This would virtually make my new position redundant before I even got started.

Fortunately for me, his suggestion was declined but he persisted and ended up with his block plants becoming the franchisee once that I had established the distribution centres.

He was looking at all four that I had been chartered with.

My first centre to establish was to be Hervey Bay on the Queensland Central Coast. Here I came face to face with the block area manager Armin.

From the very first contact with the man, it was so obvious that he treated me as inferior to himself and, was quite blatant about it in front of the staff whom he had already employed, which circumvented me.

Here where I was, armed with the selection criteria for each discipline that was required to run the centre efficiently, only to discover Armin had completed this task for me with his own criteria.

The same thing was repeated by Armin with the next centre at Rockhampton but by this time I was becoming more aware of Armin's intentions to bypass me and to take control of the distribution centres.

Finally, the Townsville and Cairns centres were also completed but things were becoming harder for me as the expected volumes for each centre were well below my forecasts because I had no effective control of the centres, thanks to Armin. My bosses failed to believe that Armin was making my job almost impossible.

It was sheer fate that I was in Bundaberg one afternoon and had a document to drop off for Armin at his office.

His secretary, who knew me quite well, informed me that Armin was not in that day as he had a change of plans at the last minute.

She also told me that the other office assistant was ill that day and was also not in and asked me if I could 'hold the fort' for about fifteen minutes while she ducked out, 'Of Course' I assured her as I sat in her chair in front of the computer monitor.

I could not help myself, I had a quick scan of her desktop computer and saw that she had closed all her files before she had left, but she had left the spreadsheet on and it was showing a list of the spreadsheet files.

Looking down the list I saw 'Fax Lists' and I clicked the mouse on it to open the file, the file was locked and the message came up 'Password Protected - Enter four-digit password'.

There was a loophole with this particular spreadsheet program that I had discovered back in the department days and I thought 'What the hell, I have plenty of time' and opened a 'New File' on the spreadsheet and typed $.$. which instantly put the program into 'programming mode' for editing, it's not a commonly known function as it is for programmers.

I then typed 'copy$ *.*"fax_lists" and then pressed enter'

The file 'Fax Lists' immediately came up on the screen, opened and unlocked and allowed me to scroll through it.

There were four groups listed as Group 1 to Group 4. I opened the Group1 file and it revealed the names of the fax recipients in that group which were only three recipients being Armin's superiors, next to the name was the fax number.

This PC was connected by cable to the printer and also to the fax machine.

I added my fax number to the list in this group, minus my name and then to the other three groups, I named the file 'test 1' and saved it, I then deleted the original 'Fax Lists' file and renamed my created 'test 1' file to 'Fax Lists' and protected the file with the password four-digit password of **** which are all wildcards, meaning that once prompted for the password, any four digits can be entered to open the file. The secretary would not realise that, and she would enter her four digits password to open the file.

There should be no suspicion that things had been altered.

I was just guessing that when she sent faxes she would enter on the fax keyboard the group number and the fax would read the file for the fax recipient numbers and not the names.

I was correct as I started to receive all the faxes that were sent to all of the four groups.

I soon discovered that my name was quite a favourite and that I was blamed for anything and everything that was happening around the four centres. I also read facsimiles that went to Armin's bosses about ways of removing me from my position. I kept all these faxes in a file for ammunition for what I knew was coming.

It was a few months after the fax find that I had to call into the Townsville centre to obtain the serial number of one set of the forklift spreader bars as there was a warranty issue.

The centre's manager who had been engaged by Armin was not at the centre that day, which seemed to be quite normal for this guy, and I asked the admin assistant to get me the equipment inventory, she had no idea of how to access it on the spreadsheet so I opened it up on her behalf and scrolled down the equipment list to find the item that I required the serial number.

Just as I found what I was looking for I noticed that a second forklift had been added to the inventory, I clicked on this and read the item description.

It nominated a four tonne Toyota forklift serial number and capital expenditure cost along with the place of purchase which was an address at Lucinda, which I noted. I then found the serial number that I had been seeking, closed the file and went into the warehouse to find my item to check the serial number.

I also looked for a second forklift, there was only one forklift at the Townsville Centre. Interesting.

On my way to Cairns the following week and as I drove past Ingham I noticed the signpost to Lucinda which made me remember the additional forklift.

I had thought at the time of seeing the forklift registered in the inventory, that Lucinda seemed to be an odd place to buy a forklift from as it was a fishing village. I decided to take a detour and go for a drive to Lucinda.

As I drove into the village of Lucinda looking for the address that was listed in the inventory I saw the company car of the Townsville centre manager parked at the address of the forklift purchase.

I thought it seemed strange and then noticed the company car of the Cairns centre manager also parked at that address.

Looking at the establishment at that address I knew that they did not sell Toyota four tonne forklifts.

I arrived in Cairns at the centre and asked the admin assistant where the manager was and she said that he was away for the day, she then became tearful and asked if she could speak to me in private.

She came out and sat in my car and told me that she has had enough of the way the centre was going, the manager and the storeman often disappeared for days and she was always covering for them and that only this morning the manager and the storeman had emptied the petty cash tin to buy beer to take with them somewhere.

Realising what was happening I called Armin and asked if he knew where his two managers were this morning, he said that they should be at the respective centres.

I did not tell him what I had found but I contacted the head office in Sydney, bypassing my superior as I had lost trust in the management system at that stage.

The result in my call was the removal of the Besser block arm of the company in operating the four centres, and the sacking of the two managers with the transfer of Armin, to, I don't know where? And have never seen him to this day!

I never did find out what became of the forklift/boat from Lucinda, but, apparently, Armin had signed off on the capital expenditure request from the Townsville manager for an additional forklift that was required to handle to extra volume of product he was forecasting.

He had then got the boat dealer at Lucinda to invoice the boat out as a Toyota Forklift. What a fucking joke

Things were now so much better without Armin and I was actually enjoying my job.

Each week I set out an itinerary which went like this, week 1: Tuesday to Thursday - Cairns

week 2: Tuesday to Thursday - Rockhampton

week 1: Tuesday to Thursday - Hervey Bay

week 1: Tuesday to Thursday - Townsville / Brisbane

The distances, other than to Cairns were too great for driving as it took a whole day plus accommodation on the way to get to Rockhampton and Hervey Bay from Townsville and the company felt it was unsafe to drive any more than seven hours in a day, so I would fly to each location and hire a car for the few days that I was there.

One Monday morning I drove from my home in Townsville up to Cairns as per my itinerary and spent the wettest week that I have ever seen and was unable to return to Townsville on the Friday due to road closures.

I waited until the following Monday and things were no better so I left my car at the centre and flew back to

Townsville and then the following day to Rockhampton, back home on Friday morning and then hired a car until I left to go to Hervey Bay on Monday.

The following week I flew to Cairns to retrieve my car and decided not to take my car to Cairns during the wet season again, I suppose that I had to learn the hard way.

I had finally franchised out all of the centres except Cairns and after another twelve months had a good prospect for a buyer at the Cains centre.

It was now 1995, I had been with the internal lining manufacturer for four years and I was spending nine nights away from home every month and I was getting fed up with it and it certainly wasn't doing my marriage any favours. The only saving thing there, was that I was earning so many Ansett frequent flyer points, that my wife could visit her parents in Sydney each month just on my points alone for her flights. I had gained Diamond status with the Anset Golden Wings Club.

I had by this stage upgraded my twenty nine foot Vancouver yacht, to a forty two foot 'John Pugh' motor sailer, but other than annual holidays, the last of which I sailed from Townsville down around the Whitsunday Islands and back in the four weeks that I had, it wasn't getting any use and the marina fees seemed to increase every year. Sadly I decided to sell my motor sailer.

It seemed that I was very committed to my work as my marina neighbour said to me when he discovered that I was selling my dream boat.

He warned me that I should still enjoy life and that I should learn to turn off from work, from time to time, to relax.

His final words were, 'There is more to life than work'.

He was so right, but I didn't listen.

The new franchisee was ready to sign up for Cairns which would help ease my workload and the week he was to take the centre over I was in Rockhampton and had an enormous deal happening with a major hardware outlet at one of their stores at Gladstone that looked like it would link to all of their outlets Australia wide.

I was staying at the hotel in Rockhampton and I had driven down to Gladstone to meet the managing director of the hardware company who had flown from Melbourne to finalise the big deal. During the afternoon I received a call from my boss Allen telling me to go to the reception at my hotel in Rockhampton to receive a very important fax, I told him that I was in Gladstone and would be there at five pm.

Allen did not know about my deal with the national hardware outlet.

The Outlets managing director's connecting flight from Brisbane to Gladstone was delayed and he would not be in Gladstone until about eight o'clock that night and he would be flying out first thing on the following day so I booked a hotel room in Gladstone and forgot all about receiving the fax from my boss Allen.

Allen had called me early the next morning and asked why I had not contacted him at five o'clock yesterday so that he could send the fax to the hotel reception. Without telling him about the hardware deal, as it was not yet finalised, I said I would be there at five o'clock, definitely, today.

He was not impressed and said that I had better call him from the hotel reception at Rockhampton at five pm that day.

The deal with the national hardware distributor went through and I had a signed supply agreement in my briefcase by ten o'clock that day and spent the remainder of the day with the local manager finalising minor issues.

This deal was in the hundreds of thousands of square metres of lining product each month.

I arrived back at the hotel in Rockhampton at five o'clock that afternoon feeling elated and was excited to inform my boss Allen, about the huge supply agreement that I had signed up on that day.

The contract had only to be ratified by the lining manufacturer and then, the national hardware company, would place immediate orders for hundreds of thousands of square metres of internal linings.

From the hotel lobby, I called Allen's mobile to say that I was in the lobby and ready to receive the fax and would break the big news to him about the supply contract. Allen answered his phone the instant it rang and gruffly asked if I was in the lobby, as soon I said yes he said good, wait there and he hung up.

I was very confused as to what was happening when all of a sudden Allen appeared in the lobby and said 'Come with me, we have to speak'.
I followed him to the quiet bar in the hotel and he ordered drinks, he seemed to me, to be very nervous as I asked, 'What the fuck is going on?'
Passing a drink to me he told me that he had to inform me that my job was no longer available now that all of my centres had been franchised and that he felt that he must tell me in person rather than by telephone.

I suspected foul play but I couldn't quite work it out, something didn't sound right to me.
Allen went on to produce a letter showing that I would be paid twenty weeks severance pay together with all other monies owing and that I would receive my company car as a bonus gift from the company and he said, 'Sign here' offering me his pen.
I was in total shock as I signed and then just looked at him, I then thought about the big news and the contract that I had and I thought 'Fuck you' as I sipped my drink, I looked at Allen and I grinned and said 'Cheers', Allen'.

Allen had suggested dinner that night at the hotel and I agreed.

During the dinner conversation, Allen had asked, 'What do you think you will do now Peter?'

'I have no idea, I am still in shock' I had responded.

'The new franchisee at Cairns is looking for someone to run the centre' Allen replied, a little too quickly which aroused my suspicions. My only response to him was,

'Really,..Goodnight' and I left and went to my room, I was flying back to Townsville the next morning.

I arrived back in Townsville around midmorning and as I no longer had a mobile telephone I did not receive the message from Fred, the new franchisee of the Cairns centre, until I had arrived home and played back the messages on the phone answering recorder, he asked me to call him urgently.

'Fuck him' I thought as I got myself a beer just as the telephone rang.

I didn't answer the call thinking that it would be Fred from Cairns and I let the answering machine handle it.

I listened as Allen's voice came through the recorder asking me to call him urgently.

I was not in the mood to call anyone back, I wasn't feeling too happy, my wife was at work and I just felt a bit sad and was enjoying a few beers. The telephone rang again, and again I let the answering machine handle the call. It was

Allen, again and again, he asked me to call him at the Brisbane office, very urgently.

It was then that I remembered that the national hardware company was to place a huge order of product this morning once that the contract, that I had in my bag, had been ratified by the manufacturer. I laughed to myself as I opened up my letter of redundancy and double checked that I had a title deed for my company car, yes it was contained in the letter. I picked up the phone and rang telephone banking and checked my bank balance but my redundancy pay had *not* yet been placed into my bank account.

My telephone rang again, and again I left it to the answering machine, this time it was Fred.

'Hello, Peter speaking'.

'Peter, it's Fred here at the Cairns centre, how are you going?'

'I'm fine Fred, how are you, are you settling in OK?' I asked, pretending that nothing had happened.

'I heard what happened Peter, pretty sad, what do you think you will do now?' Said Fred.

'What are you talking about Fred, what do you mean?' I continued.

'Oh..I,..I, heard you had been made redundant'

'Oh..that, yeah, I was thinking of getting out anyway, I have received quite a good offer in Gladstone', I lied. There was silence on the other end, 'helloo,..helloo, are you there?'

'Oh, yes Peter, I'm here, I was.., I was going to ask if you would like to work with me in Cairns' replied Fred. My telephone was telling me that I had another call coming in.

'If the money was right I might look at it Fred, come up with a package and get back to me' and I rudely hung up. My telephone rang instantly and I let the answering machine take the call.

' Hello, Peter,...Allen here, look no hard feelings old boy, you know...about yesterday. Look something has come up that I urgently need to talk to you about, can you please call me back as soon as possible, it *is* urgent, thank you'.

Again I called my telephone banking, it was now one thirty, and still no redundancy payment. 'Well, Allen', I thought out loud, 'We shall just have to wait, won't we'.

It was now four o'clock when I again called telephone banking and I was rich! Almost six months' pay in one hit was quite a large cash amount, and plus, I had the car which was worth about twenty two thousand.

I called Allen, 'Sorry I missed your call Allen' I told him trying not to laugh.

'Oh, Pete, oh thanks for calling me back'.

I told him no worries and I asked him to hold for a moment while I got another beer, I could hear him calling out through the phone as I went to the fridge laughing. 'So what can I do for you Allen' I asked.

Allen told me that a national hardware distribution company had wanted to place a huge order for internal linings today but nobody here knows anything about it,

'They are saying that you have signed them on a supply agreement and that you have all the details, is that correct Pete?'

'Yes it is, I think they were looking at around a half million square metres on today's order with more to follow in the next few days, it's a huge contract that I signed yesterday, just before our meeting'.

'Why didn't you tell me about it, for fucks sake Peter' Allen was sounding angry.

'Because I didn't have a fucking chance to tell you after you fucking 'bushwacked' me yesterday at the hotel with your bullshit about a fax and then giving me the arse, fuck you, Allen'.

'It wasn't my fault, let me explain Peter'. Allen was begging.

'I tried to tell you all about it last night and you wouldn't listen' I lied and then hung up. 'What comes around, goes around' I thought out loud just as my wife came in the door and asked me what I was saying.

I told her all about it and she didn't seem too perturbed and just asked what I going to do now for a job. I then told her about the guy in Cairns, Fred, and that I had thought that it had been a setup with Allen and Fred, and I was guessing that Fred had suggested that he would only buy the franchise if I were to run it for him, so that's how Allen, the two faced lying prick, had set it up.

I also told her that I had spoken to Fred, today and had made it sound like I wasn't really interested in working for him and suggested that he come up with a good package and get back to me. We both enjoyed a laugh and a drink.

A Move to Cairns

Fred from the Cairns centre called me again the next morning and said that rather than he put together a package, how about I go to Cairns, at his expense of course, and discuss with him, in person the position and the salary. I agreed and made a suitable day and time to go to Cairns.

Part of the plan while in Cairns was to go house hunting, but that would happen only if the franchisee had the right deal for me.

I had a meeting with Fred one morning at his home in Stratford. I had already decided that I would demand a salary that was equal to my previous salary by double the amount and include a fully maintained company sedan as well as the other usual employment benefits.

Fred introduced me to his family at his modest home and told me that he was keeping the wolves from the door with his internal linings contracting business and that he was putting all he had into this franchise, including mortgaging the family home for finance.

It was then that I decided that I could not ask for double my previous wage and put forward a figure of my previous wage plus twenty five percent plus the vehicle. Fred had thought the figure was acceptable and said he would 'Throw more money at me' when things went well.

That never did happen, I don't mean that things did not go well, things went absolutely brilliant. Fred just never 'Threw money at me'.

It was pretty easy to get the centre happening under its new owner and Fred was a quick learner but lacked business acumen with respect to trading and customer relationships. He was good on the investment side of business acumen but that would not assist an internal linings distribution business.

I had gained a very good acumen in this type of business which had commenced with my employment with the department in Canberra and from there to project management and then to internal linings application and finally to distribution and franchising. With those four backgrounds, which in some distinct, or non distinct way, all pertained to my proven experience.

The internal lining, or lining's in general, business relies heavily on building and construction activity. If there is no activity then there is no requirement for this type of product and regardless of what you do, you can not sell an unwanted product. It is not something that you can put on 'special' for a week or so.

The construction industry was at a low when Fred had bought the internal linings franchise which does not mean the end of the world, it means that one must act in a more aware, or refined manner and also seek diversion.

Fred's internal lining installation business was just getting by with a few residential walls and ceilings, although dwelling construction was also at a low, the Cairns council home approvals had risen slightly which indicated future construction growth and that now, was the time to become established with the possible future builders, not after they had commenced construction and could play the field with suppliers.

Fred had also considered that having his own lining installation business would cause other lining contractors to shop elsewhere as he was their opposition.

I used Fred's installation arm as a great advantage in acquiring other lining contractors as customers by assuring them that if they supported the centre then their builders and projects were safe from any competition from Fred's lining company. But if they were not supporting the centre, then their builders and projects would be open to negotiation by Fred's lining company. Pretty simple really.

As Fred's children became older they were introduced, naturally into his business, but sadly not from the base, that is, starting with a broom, as it were.

No, they were introduced into the business at the higher echelon stage. Fred's daughter, straight from school, had decided that a strange and undetermined number, that appeared beside products listed in the centre's stock control and pricing computer program, was in fact irrelevant and in her wisdom deleted this number from the program, resulting in a total system crash.

Fred's son who was a self taught IT expert who had run his own business and had now sold it was also at this stage onboard and had declared this computer program crash to be unretrievable and a whole new system was employed.

Fred's son, after, presumably, studying the business's profit margins had decided to incur a surcharge to customers who paid for their goods by credit card. Brilliant.

The aging of the centre's accounts was around twenty percent at thirty days, fifty percent at sixty days and the balance of thirty percent at ninety days, and there were no penalty rates attached to these.

Fred's son's idea had caused the cash flow to drop marginally as it worked out cheaper to have an account with the centre. Some things just don't work, but sadly it is by experience that these things are learned.

It was from my contracting experience that I took over Fred's lining business with also having a decreased capacity in the centre's business activities. I started work in the morning at seven o'clock and I was not leaving my office until after six o'clock in the evening as I was hoping it would be in my interest, for the business as a whole and financially for me, in the long term.

Sadly this had taken a toll on my marriage and my wife moved back to Sydney.

The Townsville and the Cairns climates had not suited her and it was in Townsville where she had contracted Ross

River Fever that her health had suffered to the extent that her doctor had warned another case of the disease could be fatal.

This, combined with my obvious neglect towards her and her health, I think was the cause for her wanting to return down south, we discussed moving south but I was not prepared to go back and that is where it ended.

Living alone in a huge house on my own at Clifton Beach did not suit me and I decided to downsize to a two bedroom unit, on the beach, but still at Clifton Beach.

Here I had no lawn to mow or swimming pool to clean, I didn't even have to take out the garbage bins and, although too late in a way, decided to finish work each afternoon at four o'clock and I started to feel better instantly. I also started to enjoy life more by going out with friends and to parties. I had learned to catch the bus into town and visit the casino, or clubs for entertainment.

It was on one of these excursions that I went to the casino and I had a great time, I had gone there quite early at around six pm and I had enjoyed a few beers, well maybe, quite a few.

It was about eight o'clock and I had just about lost all the money that I had on me and I couldn't find my Nab card, I was sure that I had left it at home on the kitchen bench near the telephone as I had paid the electricity account by phone and had used the card.

I could not draw any money from a teller machine and I had only enough money in loose change for one beer and also a fifty dollar note which was just enough for the taxi fare home. There were no more buses out there to Clifton Beach after around eight pm.

I had to make an executive decision, keep the fifty for the cab home, or invest and hopefully win enough to extend the night out, after careful consideration, I had reached a decision, fuck it, whack it into a pokie and get a win!

As it turned out, it was the wrong decision and it wasn't until after all my money was gone that I realised that I was in a bit of a mess. It was twenty four kilometres to walk back to my unit at Clifton Beach, a five and a half hour walk at best.

What, I thought, have I done, how am I going to get home, fuck!

And then, as if in a dream, someone pats me on the back and says, 'Hey Pete, ow are ya going mate?' In a broad 'pommy' accent.

I turned around and it's my friend Harry, who owns the servo at Clifton Beach.

'Harry!..Harry,' I can't describe how happy I was to see him and I think he was a bit shocked that I seemed so happy to see him. I was saved!

'Can I get a lift home with you' I asked eagerly.

'I have only just got here Pete, I have visitors from England and they wanted a night out at the casino so here we are for dinner and then a play, but I can fit you in for a lift home when we leave' Harry explained.

I couldn't believe my luck, and I asked Harry if he had a couple of hundred dollars that I could borrow, he gave me a hundred and said that's all he had, as he didn't gamble.

I took the money from Harry and I won seven hundred dollars within about an hour and paid Harry back. I then had a great evening and I didn't really want to leave when Harry had found me and said that it was time to go, but I went.

After about a year of living alone in my unit, I was invited to dinner by one of my customers, a builder, to the Cazalys AFL club in town but this time I decided to drive into town and drink very little as it could be quite awkward to get back out to Clifton Beach late at night, as I have previously mentioned.

I can't remember who it was, but at some stage during the dinner, or afterwards, someone introduced me to a very attractive lady called, Joy. I was quite stunned by her and seemed to be instantly attracted. I think the thing that took me with Joy was that she seemed to be down to earth.

I was quite engaged with Joy as everyone from the dinner started to leave and were saying 'goodbyes' and I asked Joy if I could get her a drink. She responded with a 'Beer thanks'.

I had got two beers from the bar and she asked if I played the pokies, I asked if the Pope was Italian, or something stupid and we both had a wander around playing the pokies and drinking beers. I only had three beers at the club as I was driving.

Joy had said that she was cabbing it and I suggested I give her a lift home, she finally agreed and when we got to her apartment complex she invited me in for a drink. I told her that would be a good idea but that, sadly, I could not drink anymore as I would most likely go over the limit.

Joy said that I should not take it the wrong way but that she had a spare room if I wanted to kick on drinking as we were having a great discussion about, what? I don't remember, but I do remember we drank all her beer in the unit that night and that she told me that she would be going to work at two thirty am that morning and to help myself to coffee in the morning and lock the door when I left.

I had awoken the next morning and I presumed that Joy had gone to work at two thirty that morning as she had said, as I seemed to be on my own in her unit.

In the kitchen, whilst making a coffee I saw the note she had left on the kitchen bench saying help yourself to breakfast with her telephone number included.

I called her number and after a while, she answered 'Hello, Joy speaking'.

'Good morning' I said, 'I am just leaving your unit and I will give you a call later'

'Oh,..Peter?' She said.

'Yes,..Great company and drinks last night, we should do it again. Oh…and by the way, I let your cat in'.

'I don't have a cat!' She sounded anxious.

I laughed and told her that I was only joking and then she sounded relieved and also had a laugh.

We saw each other regularly and got on very well together, we seemed to like pretty much the same things in so much as food and drink and playing the pokies, music even!

To the extent that we invariably decided to ditch one unit and live in the other one. Clifton Beach seemed to have more going for it even if it was much farther away from the city.

Being with Joy, to me was like a new lease on life, I really mean that, she had made such a difference in my outlook on life from just basically work, to enjoyment. No pun intended there!

I had told her about my sailing boats and thought that she might like to give sailing a try. She was very unsure about boats but we decided to buy a small sailboat so she could try it out.

We found a second hand Hobie Cat out at Mirriwinni, a small village north of Cairns.

I didn't have a towbar on my car and I told the guy who was selling it, that we would buy it if he could deliver it to Clifton Beach, he agreed.

The fellow brought the boat down to our unit and asked me if I had any sailing experience.

I stuck out my chest and quoted the boats that I had sailed, a Skate, a Fireball, Vancouver 29 and a John Pugh 42 foot motor sailer.

'No...No! he said, I mean Catermarans!'

'No, I have never sailed a cat' I replied.

'There is a BIG difference, they are nothing like a mono-hull sailboat, they are total.ly different' he replied and suggested that we put the boat in the water and he would give me a demo.

The closest boat ramp was Palm Cove just a short distance north of Clifton Beach and as we intended to leave the boat on the beach in front of our unit, he suggested we sail it back from Palm Cove and his wife would drive back from Palm Cove with the boat trailer to park at the unit's car park. Agreed, perfect idea.

As we pushed the Hoby Cat from the trailer into the water, the seller said that these cats don't come to life until they touch the water.

I was starting to think that this bloke was full of shit when, all of a sudden, the boat was in the water and it was! Active, it was pulling on the bow line that I was holding.

There was little breeze, perhaps three knots, if that, the man told me to sit up on the bow and that he would take the help and sheet. He then told me to 'hold on' and I thought that he must be a dick, 'hold on' I thought, like, what's going to happen, it's only a sailboat for fucks sake!

The man pulled in the sheet (the rope on the boom of the main sail) and I went flying backwards and landed on the seller.

It was unbelievable, this boat was flying, it was exhilarating and before I knew it, we were at Clifton Beach in front of our unit. Man that was *quick*. I had never experienced such a thrill on a sailboat like that before, I was most impressed.

The first weekend came up and we were both keen to try out 'the cat' We took nibbles and beers and pushed the Hobie Cat from the beach into the water and we headed off, it was brilliant and it was even quicker than my experience of the cat as the wind was a bit better. Passed a couple of power boats with ease and did a circumference of the Double Point Island and then headed across to Buchan Point Beach where we we going to stop for a beer, I looked across at Joy, she was as white as a ghost and was holding on for life, she was terrified. In my utter enjoyment of sailing the Hobie Cat, I had become enthralled and had not even thought to look across at her as I assumed that she would also be enthralled. I was wrong, she was terrified and wanted off.

We stopped at Buchan Point and had a couple of drinks and Joy had now relaxed but she wanted no part of this boat. I had explained that the boat was really the only way home from here and that I would take it slow and get her back safely. It was a slow but safe voyage back to Clifton Beach.

Work was happening but I wasn't as keen as I had been, I was losing interest in work. Work was no longer my main interest.
Joy was working two jobs when I met her and now she had jettisoned the second job and now also appeared to be enjoying life.

It was around this point that the franchisee of the Townsville centre had decided to get out of the business, Fred had become aware of this and told me that he was interested in acquiring this franchise and asked me to go down to Townsville and do a viability thing for him.
I explained to Fred that would be fine by me but I also explained that it would most likely take about a week to get the full and honest picture of the Townsville construction activity and the viability of the linings centre in the current market conditions.

Joy came with me down to Townsville and we had a great time. We stayed at the Townsville Casino Resort and enjoyed its great array of fine foods.

A trip to Magnetic Island where I showed Joy my old haunts and my former house in Picnic Street.

All this time I was still gauging the building activity. I met with the manager of the franchise, he was not the owner and he had been instructed to let me see anything that I needed to in respect to the franchise.

After spending some time with the centre's manager I had a good idea of what the main issues with the centre might be and why the franchisee wanted to quit.

We returned to Cairns following a week in Townsville. It's true, you don't know what you've got until it's gone. It was so good to get back to Cairns, there is no comparison, believe me.

Fred was keen to hear my thoughts on whether he should buy the franchise or not.

I told him outright that the way it was being run was to its detriment and that it would indeed be a very viable proposition.

Fred then told me that he was considering sending his daughter down to Townsville to run it, should he buy it, that is.

When I told him that, that would not make it a viable proposition, he became withdrawn and defensive with a 'Why would that be unviable'

'Mate, you need someone who is outgoing and personable, but most important, you need someone who knows the business, your daughter has a hell of a lot to learn yet'. I told him the truth.

'I'll send Jonno down there, he could run it'. Fred counteracted.

'Jonno!' I said, 'Jonno can hardly run the Cairns centre with me helping him. No, you need someone who has the knowledge, or keen to acquire it, someone who is honest and we both know that Jonno isn't honest'. Fred didn't like to hear that and said to me, I suppose I am the only one to go down there then.

I made his day when I told him that I would leave his employ before going down to Townsville.

The look on Fred's face was one of sheer despair. I just knew that he thought that I wanted to go to Townsville to run the centre and that I was the obvious choice, but he thought he would belittle me by suggesting the stupid idea of sending his daughter and then Jonno.

That would be like getting the village idiot to do the prime minister's job.

I had my thoughts for the Townsville job on another employee we had in the store, to me, he had all the attributes required but sadly Fred could not see that far.

As much as I have a good regard for Fred, he has no idea when it comes to staff or staff selection, absolutely, no Idea.

Sadly, I found Fred to be the type of person who after reading the preface to a book, he knew the whole story. It was so apparent when I started to teach him about how the franchise works he knew it all after a couple of months and try to make me feel that I needed him.

There were many people that he did not like and three times the number of people that did not like him.

I noticed on quite a few occasions when we would be in the store or showroom area that he would disappear when certain customers came in and I know that he closed some accounts as he did not like the people.

My former wife was always telling me that Fred was a user and that he was just using me for his own betterment.

The closest pub to where we lived was at Palm Cove, The Palm Cove Tavern.

It was about a two kilometre walk along the beach from our unit to the tavern. It was an easy walk there during the daylight, such as in the afternoon, but coming back if we had overstayed, which was not very hard to do, and it was dark, was not very easy and quite scary.

Getting from the tavern to the beach in the dark was easy, it was lit by street lights. Once on the beach and, knowing in which direction to head, was also easy as we could see the lights of Trinity Beach, the beachside suburb south of Clifton Beach. It was the pitch blackness, that lay between that we weren't sure of. You can't see Clifton Beach at night until you virtually get to it!

Not to mention that it was not uncommon for crocodiles to be on the beach.

After the first episode where the darkness had crept in with us being, totally, unaware, whilst drinking and playing pool in the tavern, of finally getting back home after stumbling in the pitch black, not being able to see each other, and were so relieved when we saw the first lights of Clifton Beach, we decided that we would never do that again. No! Fuck that!

I think it was after, about the third time, that we had ventured home on the beach in the dark, that we had decided to buy bicycles to use on our tavern excursions. These would make it so much easier to get to the tavern via the bike path from Clifton Beach to Palm Cove.

We had bought a combination bike lock so that we could lock the bikes together for security and we had asked the guy at the Palm Cove Tavern Bottle Department if we could lock them up there, to which he had agreed. That was about two o'clock in the afternoon.

We must have become quite involved in our drinks and game of pool that afternoon as it was about eight o'clock when we stumbled around to the bottle department to collect our bikes. It was a different staff member manning the bottle shop and we told him that we were collecting our bikes. After trying to unlock the combination lock without any success, the bottle shop attendant asked if we were sure that the bikes belonged to us. I finally opened the bike lock and we headed off.

Lights!....we had never even considered getting lights for our bikes and once we ran out of street lighting it was again pitch black as we headed along the bike path towards home.

It was good when a car came past us heading south as its headlights illuminated our path for a little while, enough to get our bearings, but when a car came towards us, we were dazzled and could see even less. As they say, 'You never stop learning'.

A Big Move

We had decided that unit living was good but thought that living in a house with more room and shed and garden might be better.

We were lucky to find a great house at Birdwing Place in Caravonica. It was a split level home on the hill, with four bedrooms and two bathrooms, complete with views across Stratford to the airport.

The lower level had an entrance foyer, stairs to the upper level and a double garage and storage area. There was also a door to the undercroft and a large area just waiting to be built in.

I knew the builder personally and he told me that the open area could be enclosed and connected to the entrance foyer as he had allowed in the setting out of the blockwork in that area, an entrance size in the blocks without any steel of block laps and it can be easily removed to form a two metre wide by two point one metres high doorway.

Just as soon as we had moved in, I had set about the downstairs extension.

It was going to be two rooms that were connected in an 'L' form, the first room where the large entrance would be six metres wide by six metres long and connecting to the next room of ten metres long by four meters wide. A two metre partition at the end of this room was placed for a bathroom and a utility room. The whole area was tiled in four hundred by four hundred ceramic.

The perimeter of this area was concrete masonry columns at three point six metre spacing which I filled in with mainly glass sliding sections and infills of 1.2mm x 150mm pressed metal stud and lined with 8mm fibre cement sheet externally and 13mm internal plasterboard sheet with fibreglass insulation. The external sheet I rendered to match the external blockwork.

We now had a downstairs bar, lounge, pool room, bathroom and utility room. It was magic and became our favourite area.

I was told by a good and reliable source that in 2005, somewhere in Brisbane, the owner/occupier of a new unit in a newly constructed block of medium density apartments had concerns with respect to the noise of water flushing and draining from the unit above him and although told by the builder, through the body corporate, that this was quite normal and acceptable he found the noise and the answer to his concerns to quite unacceptable and he engaged a building surveyor.

The building surveyor found that the ceiling below the waste pipes from the upper level and the partitioning in the lowered area did not comply with the respective Australian Standards with respect to sound rating.

The building surveyor also discovered that there were no fire collars installed around the PVC waste pipes at the concrete soffit and other non fire rated penetrations within the ceiling area and some non fire rated penetrations through the adjoining party walls.

The building surveyor had drawn these issues to the attention of the Queensland Building Services Authority who promptly condemned the building and ordered immediate rectification.

These defects and actions taken had echoed around the state and all branches of the QBSA were now investigating new and recently constructed unit buildings to check for Passive Fire Protection compliance. Anyone who held a Passive Fire Certifier Certificate, or Certificate of Passive Fire Accreditation was in huge demand. They were few in number, I just happened to hold one.

It was in 1994 that whispers of non compliant passive fire rated construction in walls and ceilings around Queensland were to be investigated by the QBSA.

It was that year that I studied and attained my passive fire accreditation and obtained my passive fire certifier license the following year.

It was in 2006 that a company specialising in passive fire protection certification contacted me to announce that they were looking for a passive certifier in Far North Queensland with a remuneration package attached that was impossible to refuse. I didn't refuse.

It was all very sad my leaving Fred and his family business. There was a bit of a 'send off' that had been the idea, and organised by Elise the 'Anchor lady' of the centre's reception and product order receiving, whom I had employed when I was running the centre following the sacking of the block wing on the company.

After working for Fred for eleven years I received a few beers at Dunwoodys Tavern, and that was it. It was almost like he was relieved that I was going. Cheers!

I must add at this point that I may sound a little harsh on Fred, we were, and still are very good friends. Fred tends to forget very easily, or he has a very short memory, the people who have been loyal to him and have given their all as far as dedication, and for some most of their working life without any reward other than their salary.

I can clearly remember when Elise, who was there when Fred had first taken over the centre in 1996.

Elise had asked Fred if her hours could be changed to allow her to take and collect her son from school/ It was no big ask to which Fred without any consideration, refused.

It was only a couple of years later that Fred employed an additional lady to assist Elise and when she asked Fred to adjust her work hours to suit her drop off and collection of her daughter Fred had agreed instantly. I could imagine how Elise must have felt.

In all the years that I had worked for Fred, I had received no bonus or reward whatsoever for being totally dedicated towards him.

Many people that I know refer to Fred as a dickhead, but! He is a multi millionaire these days, I'm not.
He didn't actually have the arse hanging out of his pants when I first came into contact with him at the construction site of the Reef casino, but he didn't have money to burn either, and I remember only too well the nights sitting in his dingy little office at the storage shed that he rented from a relative, as we planned how we would combine the centre with his, then present, lining contracting company. He never did 'throw' that money at me.

I started with the passive fire protection company and spent a little time down in Brisbane at one of their centres, brushing up on the latest regulations and Australian and New Zealand Standards with respect to passive fire equipment, applications and deployment, heady stuff but I soon got up to speed and became quite busy around the North and Far North Queensland region. I had no idea how much I had to learn but it was a great challenge.

My office was located at our home which boasted more than enough room. It was a great environment and felt much more relaxed and had very little or no pressure once I had got my head around things.

Joy had now moved from the high pressure, high work volume, position, that she had been committing herself tirelessly to and was now working as a Horticulturist at a retirement village with extremely flexible work hours.

This enabled Joy to come with me when I travelled around my area and she assisted me in presenting training courses to enable tradesperson to gain their passive fire installers certification.

On my way back home one afternoon, I made a diversion to the Smithfield shops, more specifically, to the bottle shop to collect a carton of beer. While I was there I also asked for a carton of Marlboro cigarettes. The young fellow who was serving me said, 'Have you thought of giving up smoking?'

'No, I have not, and what has it got to do with you?' I didn't like his question.

'Don't get me wrong', he quickly added. It's that my mum bought me this 'stop smoking program' for my birthday six months ago and I told her that it is bullshit and that these things are a con, that they don't work and are a waste of money. And to prove it, I went and did the course! And guess what, it worked, I have not smoked since and I don't even feel like a smoke'.

I was impressed! 'Tell me more', I asked and he gave me a card for the 'Stop Smoking' it said 'Laser Therapy' and had the address and phone number. I thanked him and continued home.

The lady on the phone at the laser therapy centre said 'Five hundred dollars, payable at the time of your booking'.

'What!' I said, nearly fainting. They are pretty smart, amongst the questions that they ask is 'How many cigarettes do you smoke a day and what brand'? And then, when you get a shock from the price that they quote you, they say,

'But that is only a month's supply of cigarettes'.

I arrived there at the appointed time, I had already paid my five hundred dollars up front and I was pretty convinced that I had just blown five hundred bucks! 'What the fuck is wrong with me'? I was thinking as I went into the treatment room. And removed my shoes, yes! My shoes. The man told me to lie on the table and relax as he placed magnets behind my ears and commenced to point his little laser beam between my fingers, he didn't stop talking.

'So Peter, you used to smoke Marlboro, me too! They were great cigarettes, I loved them but I was smoking a lot more than you at twenty each day, I was smoking forty to fifty some days, it depended on how long I would stay up for at night. If I was watching a really good movie I would probably smoke half a pack watching just that'. And he went on ...and on... and, before I knew it he was equipping me with a bottle of water, some yellow pills and a strong rubber band.

The man told me to wear the rubber band on my right wrist at all times and to carry the bottle of water with me wherever I go. He then said that if a felt like a smoke, snap the rubber band on my right wrist with my left hand and then take a drink out of the water bottle.

I looked at him blankly and said 'You *are* fucking joking, aren't you?'

He just smiled and said 'You'll see'.

And I have never smoked since that day, true!

Anyway, Joy had said that I could buy a new car if I stopped smoking, it was a form of incentive and the money I was saving in not buying cigarettes would almost pay the monthly payment for the new car.

I wanted a 78 series Landcruiser RV, we had gone down to the Toyota dealer and he had the latest model, or I should say, the last model of the 78 series in a GXL model, it was gold in colour and he said that there were no more of the model that I wanted, the RV, as Toyota had stopped making this series and that the new V8 series would follow soon.

He worked out a 'good' price for us at sixty thousand dollars neat. We had another look at it, the tray on the back was aluminium and looked cheap It didn't come with a bull bar it was very basic and the interior was almost identical to the 1973 FJ model Landcruiser short wheelbase 'Rag Top' that I used to have, that I paid five thousand seven hundred dollars for.

This one didn't even have a fucking air conditioning unit, for sixty fucking, thousand dollars. We told him that we would look around and he could not care less if we bought it from him or not.

Someone had mentioned the Toyota dealer in Innisfail so I gave them a call. I told the feller on the other end of the phone what I was looking for and to my amazement said that he only had a demo one, it's an RV with a steel tray and it's done around six thousand Kays and it's mine for sixty six thousand dollars, out the door with rego.

We were in Innisfail just two hours later looking at a Midnight Blue RV 78 series, including the tray, bull bar on the front, air conditioning, electric windows and carpet on the floor, Wow! We bought it. 'This is the last of the good ones', the salesman had said, 'They're not making this series anymore'. We were pretty stoked as we drove it back to Cairns.

We now had two Landcruisers, the 100 series wagon that Joy drove and the 78 series ute.
We had seen the slide on caravan/camper setups and we had started to look at them with a view of getting a second hand one for camping trips around the area.
It was a Saturday at around seven o'clock in the morning when I received a call to say my father was pretty crook in hospital and he might not be coming out.

We decided to take the RV for a drive to Brisbane to visit my father, who had recovered somewhat by the time we had arrived in Brisbane.

We had a look around Brissy for the slide on caravans while we were down the and found a pretty old one for five thousand dollars which we put on the back and brought home with us.

We called it Tardi, after the Tardis on Doctor Who.

It really changed the way the Landcruiser handled on the road, it felt unsafe on corners and I drove it back at about ninety kilometres per hour max. Once we got it home I had airbags installed on the cruiser's rear suspension and it didn't even know the slide on was on its back.

We stripped the little slide on and changed it around a bit and painted it Midnight Blue to match the ute. It looked better than what it was, but it was a lot of fun for the price.

We even loaned it to Joy's sister and her husband who took it around the north for a few weeks and they loved it. Life was just brilliant and we were loving it! And we still are to this day.

Joy had dedicated her time to take part in the 2007 inaugural Cardiac Challenge bike ride from Cairns to Cooktown. It was a three hundred and thirty three kilometre, three day bike ride.

I went along with 'Tardi' out slide on caravan/camper as her support crew and had a ball.

I was so proud of her as she completed the ride on her 'K Mart' bicycle competing against others on their thousand dollar plus pushies and finishing with equal with most of them. And I am still very proud of her for so many things.

It was 2008, and we received a very unexpected invitation to Fred's sixtieth birthday party at his newly constructed mansion.

I was under the impression that it was more of a housewarming, look at me!..look at me! type of party rather than a birthday.

Anyhow, Fred, I think, was using this opportunity to find out if things were good with me in the passive fire industry and he asked me to call into his office for a chat sometime, like 'next week would be good'.

His new home was very impressive and certainly displayed the fact that he was very wealthy.

Fred told me that the Townsville centre was fucked! I continued to eat my fish and chips from the cardboard takeaway container as I listened to him, 'Fred had shouted lunch'.

He didn't seem too pleased when I didn't appear to be too surprised and I hunched my shoulders and also stated it verbally. 'Well, Jonno was still running it!'

Fred asked me if I could take it on and fix it or he would shut it down, he admitted that he couldn't sell it, as there was nothing to sell. I told Fred that I would look at it,

I would take a trip to Townsville and check out the situation, and he could cover the bill.

I was due to do a passive fire course in Townsville anyway but Fred didn't need to know that.

I hadn't seen Jonno in quite a while and as I observed him lounging in his well appointed office I didn't think he had changed much other than stacking on the weight. He had suggested that I buy him lunch at the pub down the road and as we were leaving his office, his daughter, who was also working at the centre was just coming into the office, 'You remember Kyle' Jonno had said.

'I certainly do, how are you Kyle, would you care for lunch with us' I had asked.

'Lunch!..lunch, what's lunch, no, I am far too busy for that', she didn't even say hello. She then asked her father something and then left.

Jonno locked his office as we left, I noticed that he did not acknowledge the office staff as we did so.

Jonno took his car as he said he would be going elsewhere after lunch and would not be returning to his office.

The conversation over a steak and a couple of beers was mainly about how busy Jonno was and how good his new company Ford X8 car was and how much volume he, was pumping through the centre.

Following lunch, I called back at the centre and discovered that Kyle was not there and was told that she would not be back that day. I was talking to a girl called Leila, she was working at the Cairns centre for a while and moved down to Townsville as he boyfriend was in the army based at Laverack Barracks.

I had noticed that there seemed to be a lot of staff in the office, like five people all up and three people working in the store together with Jackson, who I had met when he was the former centre manager when Fred had bought the store.

He told me that Fred had offered him the job as the storeman which suited him and with a good salary.

Jackson told me that he started every morning at six o'clock, opening time and finished at five o'clock, closing time. He said that they were all big days with the big volume going out each day and that they had two subcontract trucks, each with a driver and offsider to do the deliveries.

He also told me that Jonno did not normally arrive at his office until around eleven o'clock each morning and was normally gone by about two o'clock each afternoon and it was pretty much the same with Jonno's daughter except she maybe spent less time at the centre.

Well I was quite surprised, I had half expected to see a sleepy centre with people just lolling around waiting for an order to come in for something to do, certainly not the case. Here it was, according to everyone that I spoke with, 'flat out'.

If Fred was going broke, then something was gravely wrong and the only way to find out would be to do an audit, I called Fred and suggested I commence an audit and it sounded to me like Fred had shat himself and told me that an audit would be out of the question as Jonno would get the shits.

I reminded Fred that he had sent me down here to look at the place and now he was worried about me asking questions at the centre and delving into the sales and margins, Fred suggested that I slow down and get back to him with an answer on whether I will take it on or not.

I put together a proposal to Fred, for Joy and myself to take control of Townsville on a subcontract and he jumped at the deal.

I told my employer that I was leaving their employ, but not to leave them in a bind I said that I would still complete some inspections for them as well as complete training courses that were already booked. All was sweet with them.

Return to Townsville

I had told Fred that I would go to Townsville and sack Jonno and his daughter and would remove them from the property on the spot in order to prevent them from touching any of the computers and records. Fred agreed.

I had spoken to Jackson and told him that I was about to get rid of the management and I asked for his assistance, he was one hundred percent behind me, I told Jackson that following that I would be taking over the centre and that he would be employed as the assistant manager.

Jackson was thrilled with both prospects, disposing of the management and he becoming management.

I had planned with Fred and Jackson that I would go to the Centre the next Monday at eleven o'clock, as that seemed the time that both Jonno and Kyle would be present.

As I walked into the centre on that day Jonno was in his office with, I assumed a customer, and Kyle was in the adjacent office. As I approached Kyle she quite rudely said that she didn't have time to speak with me as she was so busy.

I went into her office anyway and told he to stop whatever it was she was doing and to pack her things as she was no longer employed here.

She just gave me a blank look and then walked into her father's office and closed the office door, with whoever was also in the office with her father. I tried to open the office door, it was locked.

My mobile rang, it was Fred telling me that I had upset Jonno and Kyle and that they would leave on their own free will by Friday.

I told Fred that he must be fucking joking and that they needed to be gone today as we had planned. Fred reiterated that Jonno and Kyle could stay there until Friday.

I could not believe it, I advised Jackson that he would be in charge of the centre until I returned the following Monday and I filled him in on what was happening with Jonno and Kyle, he was as confused as I was.

I really believe that Jonno had something over Fred, maybe a picture of him rooting a goat, I don't, but at this stage, I had nothing to lose and I spent the week with Joy looking for a house.

We looked at a really nice four bedroom house on the beach in Jamaica Cresent at Bushland Beach, it had a great swimming pool and outdoor BBQ area and the back gate walking onto the beach.

It was for rent and would be for sale following a six month term of rental, we said that we would take it.

Returning to Cairns we organised for a removalist and a real estate property rental agent and had moved into Bushland Beach by the following Monday and While Joy got the house sorted I was at the centre trying to sort out the mess. I won't go into detail here as it would not be appropriate but probably needless to say the business was in quite a mess.

Within six months the centre's staff had been reduced to five reception and warehouse personnel and three people for the deliveries on the two trucks that we now had.

The centre's output volume had, by design, decreased by forty percent and we were in business and making a profit.

Many of the local lining tradespeople had given the centre a wide berth as the centre was dealing directly with the builders and circumventing the tradies. This resulted in lining sales but all ancillary item sales were lost as it was the tradie that purchased these and the ancillary items had the greater margin.

But I was well on the way to rectifying this major issue.

I had approached the builders and convinced them to let the installer also supply the product, as he did with his sparkie and plumber, in return I would supply to them free of charge enough internal linings for one 'display home' within so many homes, as per a ratio, if they specified that their contractor was to use my product. Win-win for the builder.

This would force the lining contractor to purchase the product from me, but I had to get a better relationship with him if I wanted him to also buy from me, all the products required to complete the lining project.

I had organised for the 'Townsville Masters' golf day to be on a Friday morning and had provided two months' notice of the event.

The tickets to participate were on sale at the centre at Fifty dollars per head and limited numbers to a maximum of fifty two players.

'Bullshit! Fifty bucks to go to a golf day, fuck off' was said by more than one tradie who had been into our centre and noticed the 'golf day' sign. Nevertheless, all the tickets were sold well within the two months before the day.

The advertisement had stated that the fifty dollars included;

18 holes of golf including fees.

1/2 share of golf buggy.

Breakfast at 7 am of bacon and egg muffins served with rum and bonox.

Lunch of barbequed rump steak and salad with bread rolls.

Six drink tickets for exchange of one can of beer or soft drink of choice.

I had also advertised that the first prize would be an Engel fridge valued at one thousand, twelve hundred dollars plus many other prizes and giveaways.

I had contacted various suppliers of trade tools and other items used in walls and ceilings and offered 'Tees' for sale at one thousand dollars each.

The idea was that the supplier would set up a marque at their Tee and promote their products to the Tradies as they tee'd off.

I had eighteen for sale but was happy to sell only five. The sponsor would be getting fifty two possible customers at their tee on that day.

One sponsor who was very keen was the local Mitsubishi dealer, he saw the value in so many possible links for new vehicles and was serving up tot's of rum for all his Tee visitors.

Another Sponsor from an insulation company was serving up 'Jägerbomb's, it's a bomb mixed drink made by dropping a shot of Jägermeister into an energy drink, typically Red Bull. This ended up being the busiest Tee on the course.

The food, drinks, golf fees, golf buggies were all covered with the entry fee and I had five thousand dollars from the sponsors to spend on trophies, gifts and giveaways.

The day was a huge success and we had the next golf day for the following year booked out six months in advance and had to find a bigger venue with more golf buggies to accommodate more players, which equalled more customers for our centre.

Following the first twelve months of new management and direction, the centre was showing a very healthy net profit which also meant a very healthy percentage based bonus for the staff and a nice share of the net for us plus our contract value. Everyone was happy.

The rental property at Jamaica Cresent that we were looking forward to buying was a very nice home. The day we looked at it was a beautiful early morning at around eight o'clock, the morning sun was shining and there was only a gentle breeze. It was late winter and one of those days you wish for, just perfect.
As the days were getting longer with summer on its way, the winds were getting stronger and it was now impossible to light the BBQ near the pool, and the pool, it was just too windy to go swimming, it was unpleasant with the constant buffering of the wind.

The wind eased in the late afternoon's and out came the sandflies, and the mosquitos. It was impossible to be outside without being bitten by either sandflies or mosquitoes.
The clothing that was hanging on the clothesline for drying would attract mosquitoes and unseen they would be transported into the house on the clothing and we would be bitten inside the house as well as outside, it was becoming a nightmare and following our six months of renting we declined to purchase the house.

We had quiet neighbours beside us, next to a shed, which we eventually found out was their garage. It was one weekend that was overcast and drizzling rain, not a very warm day at all, that I could hear the neighbours next door swimming in their pool, I just assumed that they were either very keen or that maybe they had southern visitors. After some time I could hear, what I thought to be, younger voices laughing and more splashing or swimming sounds.

It was a little later that the neighbour's blue Ford sedan came down their driveway,

I was out at the front at that stage for some reason or other and I waved at them as they drove past, not really looking at them, just a quick wave.

I suppose it was about a week later when the police knocked on our door and asked if we had heard anything happening at next door.

As it turned out, the neighbours were away and someone had broken into their home during the weekend and caused a lot of damage.

I told the police that I had heard people swimming in the pool on one day that weekend and just assumed that it was them. The police told me that the people who broke into the home were not swimming, but were throwing furniture from the upper level balcony, down into the pool.

I felt pretty bad when I heard that their blue Ford sedan was also stolen as I had waved to the occupants.

We both had bicycles that we had brought with us from Cairns and during a pleasant ride along the Mount Low Parkway we rode down Frendon Parade, just exploring, and we came across an attractive looking home that was displaying a 'for sale' sign.

We stopped our bikes on a vacant, tree covered block, that was opposite the house that was for sale and we took drinks out of our pack and rested on the vacant block of land.

After a little while a lady approached us asking if we were alright, and then informing us that we were on private property.

We apologised to the lady and said that we were just taking a break having ridden from Bushland Beach. She said 'That's fine, take your time, I was just checking to see if you were alright'.

'We are fine, that's a nice looking house over the road' I said indicating to the house that was on the market.

'It's a beautiful home, are you looking to buy a house around here' she asked.

We told her about the sandflies, mozzies and the wind where we were presently living, and she said that the place was famous for sandflies on the mudflats at the beach and that for many years no one built on the beachside of the road exactly for that reason, but now there are new houses built all along there. I now remembered that I brought my dogs here to swim the last time that I lived In Townsville, and there were no houses then, there were beachside blocks of land for sale at thirty thousand dollars each that we thought was a ripoff.

We contacted the real estate agent who said that she actually had a viewing on the next day and that we could look at the home then.

We liked the home and bought it, we couldn't get out of Jamaica Cresent quickly enough.

Our new home was on acreage, as with the surrounding homes so we had lots to do around the property.

To keep the centre's customers focused on the centre, approximately five months following the very successful golf day, I started a new campaign and called it, 'The Tradies Trailer'.

I bought a seven foot by five foot galvanised box trailer with a lockable galvanised steel canopy complete with ladder rack. On this, I placed an attractive sign, 'Win This Trailer By Getting Your Gear Here' and this trailer was parked out the front of the centre each morning where it could not be missed by anyone driving down the busy road in front.

The details of how to win were also on a smaller sign attached to the trailer for anyone who stopped and looked.

The simple details were, any purchase of plasterboard fixing and setting compounds to the value of one hundred dollars would attract one ticket in the trailer raffle, so if a customer bought three hundred dollars of those items then they would receive three tickets.

Plus there were to be ten consolation prizes, a 'Ticket Holder Only' steak BBQ lunch and drinks supplied at the draw.

The centre's setting compound and fixing screws sales went through the roof. I had also organised the compound setting manufacturers to sponsor the trailer, which they did, and tools suppliers for compound tools such as trowels, screw guns, sanding machines etcetera.

For the draw day, I had closed the centre at midday as I had been advertising and I had a security guard at the front gates who would allow entry to ticket holders only.

The centre was packed and I had to order a delivery of more cold beer.

There was to be a total of ten draws for ten prizes, the major prize of course being the trailer, the other prizes were various items of tools and/or tool packages in excess of five hundred dollars each. Each prize displayed a number between one and ten.

To win the trailer, or a prize. A ticket, displaying the holder's name, was drawn from the barrel. That person then had to draw an envelope that contained a number between one and ten and win the corresponding prize.

This event proved so successful that I announced that would become an annual event, much to the cheer of the crowd.

This event had extended the centre's customer base and increased its sales of ancillary products.

These two annual promotional events that I had created were more than enough to keep customer interest at the centre, they were now annual events that every customer remembered, and you can't do better than that as far as customer relations go.

I was also aware, and it was always my top priority that I needed to ensure all of my customers were receiving a first class product and at competitive pricing. I was also aware they required first class service and for that reason, I employed the best paid and looked after delivery drivers and offsiders. A fact that is often ignored by so many businesses of today.

The delivery guys are the business's last touch with the item that has been sold to the customer.

It doesn't matter how good the deal has been or how good the product is, if these guys do not deliver the product satisfactorily, then the whole deal is lost and maybe, the customer also!

These two promotional events earned me accolades at national franchise conferences and buyer group events.

It was 2012 and the franchisor was putting pressure on Fred for more presence in the town of Mackay, we had a reseller in Mackay whom I had established and visited on regular occasions but the volume of product moved by the hardware company was very ordinary.

Both myself and Fred paid a visit to Mackay to have a look at what was happening in the area and I put forward a suggestion to Fred that we set up a centre in Mackay, Fred agreed and I approached the hardware company that was on selling our products with the idea that, If I have a centre in their town, they still maintain their lining sales, but that I would supply deliver them which meant more room for them in their store and less stock expenditure. They were rapped.

We had returned back to Townsville on the Friday night and Fred asked me if I could get some projected figures for him by Monday, which I did and the figure also showed my contract fees for a three year operational contract.

Fred decided not to open a centre in Mackay.

Tablelands

As fixed term deposits were looking good at nine percent in 2012 we decided to sell two of our rental homes, and together with an inheritance we had gained, buy a property on the Atherton Tablelands, we still had income from another rental property and that, combined with an annual term deposit payment, we decided to retire.

Fred's reaction when I told him that I was getting out was a very, 'couldn't care less', attitude.

Fred continued to operate that centre and also reversed his decision to open a centre in Mackay.

After a while, he closed the Mackay centre and then the Townsville centre. Who cares!

We had bought a lovely home on five acres of, park like gardens, and we just loved maintaining it, we called it 'The Park'.

Travelling around Australia had been on our minds for quite some time and now it seemed would be the opportunity.

We had been debating whether to buy a caravan or a motorhome and we had decided to look at caravans, we had a modest budget in mind and set off down to Cairns to check them out.

We started looking at new caravans at around the budget that we had set and we increased that budget every time we looked at the next upmarket caravan until Joy decided on the one that she wanted at around one hundred and twenty thousand dollars, it was nice and certainly had everything in it that anyone would want and we decided that it was the one for us.

'We have a problem Housten' as the saying went. The vehicle that we had intended to tow the caravan with, a 2012 Toyota SR5 Hilux was too small to tow this big caravan that we had selected, and would most likely cost another hundred thousand dollars to buy a suitable vehicle. We decided to have a look at motorhomes.

Not much to look at around Cairns insomuch as motorhomes but we had looked at the Sunliner range of motorhomes on the web and decided to visit a Queensland dealer in Brisbane. We were very impressed by the quality of their product and decided to place an order for the model that we wanted with a configuration that we thought would work.

The salesman took our order and made suggestions for inclusions and exclusions.

One item that I wanted was the Mercedes 519 v6 base for the build and the salesman suggested that I could save us around sixteen thousand dollars if we used an Iveco 4 cyl base for the build.

I was not impressed by his suggestion of an inferior type of vehicle when he had been spruiking the quality of their products.

One main item in our criteria for the motorhome was that it must be under the four point five tons weight. This was to avoid various requirements for heavy vehicles with respect to vehicle registration. We were assured that it would be under that weight.

We paid our deposit for our motorhome and we were told that it would be available for collection in Brisbane in March, a full four months for construction.

In February we received a call from the dealer to tell us that there were delays in the motorhome due to the unavailability of some materials.

In early March we again received a call from the dealer telling us that the slide out BBQ that we had ordered to be installed on the motorhome would not fit the Mercedes chassis, but that if we changed to Iveco it would be fine.

I now had suspicions about this dealer, how could they change the vehicle so late in the motorhome's production stage? I reiterated to the salesman that we wanted a Mercedes, end of story, I then told him not to worry about it,

'Don't worry about the BBQ, ok', the salesman said.

'No, don't worry about the motorhome' I said, 'we'll go elsewhere!'

'You can't, its almost completed'

'You just told me that I can change the vehicle type' I reminded him.

'No, no that was my mistake, I'll make sure the BBQ goes in'. He said and then I hung up on him. The dealership later confirmed the pickup date for the motorhome to be April 26th.

April came and a granddaughter was competing in national horse jumping at Gatton in late April, we thought that we could combine the collection of the motorhome with this equestrian event, it seemed to be perfect timing.

    I was about to book our flights from Cairns to Brisbane to collect the motorhome but thought that I might just confirm with the dealer that the motorhome would in fact be available for collection on that Friday afternoon.

The dealer assured me that it would be ready and waiting on that Friday afternoon at two o'clock.

He added that if there was a delay in the transportation of the motorhome, then he would come in personally on the following Saturday and have it ready to go on the Saturday afternoon. Great.

    Again I was about to book flights, again I had doubts about the salesman's 'overconfident' attitude and I looked up the telephone number of the motorhome manufacturer in Bayswater, Victoria.

I told the lady at the motorhome manufacturing company reception that we were to collect our motorhome from their dealership in Brisbane on the 26th of April and that I would just like to confirm that it would be leaving the factory in time to arrive in Brisbane on, or about, that date and I gave her the order number and reference number that I had been quoted when purchasing the motorhome.

The lady was very polite and friendly and asked me to hold for a while and she would check with the despatch section.

I had been waiting for a considerable time when a male voice came on the line.

'Mr Harris?' This is the managing director of this company, we have not yet started to build your motorhome. The Queensland dealer was told when he placed the order that the completion date would be June'.

I immediately called the Queensland dealer and spoke to the salesman who had only minutes earlier had assured me that I could go ahead and book flights to collect the motorhome from Brisbane. He calmly said to me that the factory may have stuffed up and that he would get back to me.

We were about to pull the pin on this dealership and look elsewhere, which was pretty sad as we had now waited over six months for the motorhome to be built and none of the other motorhome manufacturers had standard models that really suited us and all were quoting four to six months to build custom motorhomes.

The dealer called back and apologised, but blamed the manufacturer, and gave us a date in June and suggested that we collect the motorhome from Victoria for expediency and that they would pay for flights and accommodation to travel to the factory and also give us back money to cover fuel for the return trip to Cairns. After some thought, we agreed.

The dealer had also flown to Melbourne and hired a car to collect us at the airport and transport us to the hotel where we would be staying for the night and then collecting the motorhome the next morning.

I really had to question the mentality of this salesman. He knew we were arriving to pick up a motorhome that we were going to drive back to Cairns, a drive of nearly three thousand kilometres, a comfortable seven days drive with six overnight stays. So we would require some bedding, towels and other items that we would most likely buy before leaving.

But surely he would have assumed that we would need personal items including clothing for a full seven days or even more. So it would not be out of the question to expect that we would each have a sizeable suitcase. If only one each?

Then why? would this salesman hire a Nissan Micra sedan, it defied all logic and it looked like two trips would be required to ferry us and our gear, plus this 'dickhead' and his gear to the hotel at Bayswater, some fifty kilometres. We ended up having to sit on top of our bags. Unbelievable!

The next morning there was, of course, some holdup and the collection time of the motorhome was moved from nine o'clock in the morning to two o'clock in the afternoon, our illustrious salesman's flight was at three o'clock and apologised that he would not be able to go through the procedures of the motorhome with us, but he would get someone else from the factory to do that. we finally went through the procedures of receiving the motorhome and it was almost six o'clock in the evening when we left, in the dark, Bayswater and headed towards Joy's sister's house at Safety Beach.

Of course, it wasn't until we left that we discovered the Mercedes onboard GPS would not work so a detour was made to a 'Supercheap' auto shop to buy a portable car GPS as we had no idea of where we were.
The next day we went to Anaconda and bought a pair of folding chairs and a small table, then to Bunnings for a hose and a fifteen amp lead.
We were set to head back to Cairns to get everything sorted out and then a shakedown trip to Darwin.

It was all going nice, we were heading up the Hume Highway, apparently the best thing that comes out of Melbourne, when Joy heard the beep beep sound coming from the fridge which was now turned to the twelve volt setting.
The beep beep was telling us that the fridge was not working on the twelve volt setting so we placed a call to our favourite salesman at the Queensland dealership.

I'll call him Ben, I really can't remember his name, answered the phone and basically told us that we were idiots and that he was sure that we had not changed it over from two forty to twelve volts before we had left and asked us to double check and we could call him back.

I told Ben, to hang on and I pulled off the road and checked the fridge settings and told him everything was done by the book and that the fridge was beeping and it was not cold inside, how plain was that?

He said he would call us back, which he did after about one hour. We had told him earlier that we were travelling on the Hume towards Albury and he now told us that he had made arrangements with the dealership at Albury to have a look at the fridge.

The people at the Albury dealership were great and checked it all out and thought that it may have been loose connections and that all was now well. We had just gotten back onto the Hume to exit Albury when the fridge again started its, now familiar, beeping. We could not be bothered to turn back and kept on to our next stop which was Yass. We contacted Ben and told him all about the fridge. He asked us to call into their yard at the Sunshine Coast and that *they* would fix the fridge.

Between Yass and the Sunshine Coast, I left the fridge operating on gas. We don't drink hot beer.

Ben said to follow him in our motorhome and we went to the local Dometic installation people and had to leave it there for the day, Ben dropped us off at a shopping mall and said he would pick us up later that afternoon to collect the motorhome.

When collecting the motorhome later that day, I overheard the Dometic technician saying something about incorrect installation, it had now been rectified and all should be good.

We listened to the beeping again somewhere between Rockhampton and Mackay and again we reverted to gas.

I was pretty pissed off with the GPS and the fridge and the dealership had said they would rectify it one way or another and suggested that I bring it back, like drive it the sixteen hundred kilometres as if it was next door, Yeah! Right.

The Mercedes Benz dealer in Cairns repaired the GPS and reported that it had been disconnected when the motor home was constructed on it and then, incorrectly reconnected.

I had ordered a 'Smart Bar' to be installed on the motorhome and the nearest installer for that was in Mareeba, only about thirty kilometres away. While the motorhome was being fitted with the bar, the installer, who was an auto electrician, had noticed how the refrigerator was installed incorrectly and had contacted the motorhome dealership who, in turn, authorised him to repair the fridge and we never had any more problems with it.

We had packed up and enjoyed a trip to Darwin and back, we met many other people also travelling in motorhomes and caravans and had invited them to call into our property if they happened to be in the area. We had a fantastic trip and after arriving back home we discovered that we didn't have anywhere that was suitable, in all of our acreage, to park the motorhome so we had a shed erected that would double as a workshop and motorhome garage. This now meant that I could move my workshop from the attached area to a granny flat that we had and turn that area into a games room, complete with a huge screen television, a pool table and a pianola, not to mention a bar. It just got better.

We also realised that if we had visitors with motorhomes or caravans, we had nowhere for them to park. Our property being of a strange shape, did have a horse paddock, complete with stable and tack room, that also had its own entry on a different road.

I levelled off the block, which was about an acre, and made four powered sites and five unpowered sites and had electricity brought down to the stables

I converted the stables into two bathrooms which included a shower, vanity and toilet in each and also a laundry area.

The tack room I converted to a 'camp kitchen' complete with a large kitchen sink and draining boards, table and seating for eight and a large six burner BBQ.

I also made a fire pit and two other large tables and chairs.

It looked great and it was designed with family and friends in mind and had a very small fee of $20 per night for a powered site and $10 for an unpowered site, but some friends who stayed there had told other people how good it was and before we knew it, it was on Wiki Camps, and we were booked out every night and it seemed that we had made rocks for our own backs as we became so busy.

We had a huge swimming pool and we made that available for our guests, as with the games room, which we named, 'The Park Country Club' we had the big two glass door fridge loaded with various types of beer in stubbies and canned soft drink with a sign on a large glass jar, 'Beer $5 Soft Drink $5 and each day I would fill the fridge and count the money, it was *never* short but on most days was up a dollar or two. We ended up doing the same with chips and nuts which seemed to make the place more popular.

We found nearly all the people who stayed were friendly and we enjoyed their company, but sadly there is that small element that have to spoil things, such as stealing the toilet paper, the paper towel rolls and even the firewood. Some would complain that the camping fees were too much for this type of setup, others would make a lot of noise or would not clean up after themselves in the kitchen or around the fire pit.

I am a very cool-headed person, usually, and it would take a lot to get me going, but I remember one afternoon when a few people were arriving and I was in the park when an elderly couple arrived and the usual reversing procedure was happening, the woman was helping the man reverse into the site with hand signals.

I had walked over and also assisted with some hand signals and advice, when the man jumped from the car and told me, in a very rude tone, to go away and not to help him because I was making it harder for him to back his caravan into the space. I thought fair enough and left them to it, then the woman came up to me and asked me if I had an EFTPOS machine, I reminded her that it was cash only and that it was also advised cash only on the Wiki Camps and now others that were promoting the small camp. She told me that she had only a credit card and asked me in a very unpolite way of what I would suggest, as if it were my fault and that I was the one to blame,

'So, I don't have any cash, I have only a credit card, so now what should I do? She said.

'Well madam', I said calmly, 'I suggest you and your husband, get back into your car, and then, fuck off'. She stared at me as though I had poured a bucket of cold water over the top of her head, she turned on her heel and went back to where her husband was starting to set up their caravan. They were gone five minutes later. I didn't want people like that on our park.

I had to laugh at some of the campers, especially the ones who depended on solar and did not require power. When it had been cloudy for most of the day, later that night I would walk quietly down to the park with my torch often to find the solar people had an extension lead running from their camp, or caravan, to the camp kitchen power outlet. I would unplug this and the person would come out and see me, telling me they were going to pay me extra for power when they saw me in the morning. I would then accept the extra $10 and plug them back in. I often wondered if they would have told me the next morning.

We had a septic tank at the camping ground and I had also installed a 'dump point' to avoid the mess that some of them would make when attempting to empty their toilet cassettes into the bathroom toilets.

I said to people who wished to use this 'free' facility that they could only use it if they were using dedicated toilet cassette chemicals in their caravan toilets. A pretty simple request, as we had on occasions experienced the septic tanks enzyme being killed by some chemicals containing sodium percarbonate that people would use as a cheap alternative to the real thing. The smell was unpleasant for all at the camp when that happened.

The excuses that people would come up with such as, 'We mix a little eucalyptus oil with a little nappisan and it works fine, we have been doing it for years without any problems'

'Yes', I would agree, 'You don't have problems, but the poor bloke who owns the septic tank does a few days after you are gone'. They would argue for hours if you would let them, just to save fifty cents or so. I started to lose interest in them, I'm afraid.

As I said nearly all the people are good but sadly the few that just winge or bitch or want everything for nothing, give the caravan people a bad name.

We have seen people with a caravan valued in the hundred thousand dollar range with equal value tow vehicle, stealing toilet paper. I kid you not!

We were just about packed and ready to head off to Adelaide and there had been quite a lot of controversy with respect to caravan and motorhome weights which suggested that quite a large percentage of these were overweight and that the police and other authorities would be randomly checking the weights of these vehicles.

It was a hefty fine to be caught overloaded and your vehicle could not be moved from the spot where it was found to be overweight until it was brought back to the correct weight as per specifications.

Just to be sure I had taken our motorhome over the scales at the local quarry and I was guessing that we would be around three point nine tonnes, giving us an additional allowable weight of six hundred kilograms for food, drinks, water and fuel. We were shocked to find our motorhome weighed four point four tonne, we were already close to being overweight. I had calculated the weight using the weighbridge slip that the manufacturer had issued me on collection of the motorhome, I now looked carefully at the weighbridge ticket and it is my opinion that they used a ticket from a motorhome of the same build type as a generic weight certificate that was only an approximation of the weight of our motorhome.

The dealer, when I questioned this denied it.

We then took the motorhome to an automotive engineer in Atherton who did a reassessment and certified the motorhome to be compliant up to five point two tonnes gross weight and attached the required label for five hundred dollars.

We then had to re register the motorhome as a heavy vehicle and pay the additional fees.

So about a thousand dollars later we were again ready for our Adelaide trip.

We had a 'grey nomad' in the form of a Scotsman who had parked his motorhome in the park in return for caretaking duties while we were away.

We enjoyed a trouble free trip and returned after a couple of months to find that the park had barely any visitors. The Scotsman had handed over the camping fees that he had collected, it would not have been one hundred dollars in nearly two months that we had been away. It did seem strange and the Scotsman was in a hurry to leave.

During that period we had a middle aged couple that was renting out our one bedroom unit, or granny flat. They were also Scottish people but they did not get on with the caretaker Scot at all, and they told us that he had the gate entry to the camping area locked all the time we were gone.

From time to time we had other people look after the park while we were away but it did not seem to work out, something was always wrong and we receive phone calls from them saying that something was not working or that something was broken.

Once we returned from a trip, it seemed to take us a month of hard work to get the place back in order and so it got to the stage that we stopped going on trips in our motorhome.

Clockwise around Australia

We had reluctantly come to realise that our 'Park' was becoming too much for us with its upkeep and maintenance and it didn't seem that we could go travelling while we still had it, sadly we put the Park on the market.

I had been looking at properties, homes, in the Bundaberg region which for some strange reason had attracted me to it.

Geographically its location was good for our grown children, who seem to be scattered around, to visit us and it would be a good base for travelling in the motorhome as the home we were buying had very little yard maintenance and was also safe and secure.

It was a huge mansion of a place that I loved but it had so many windows it took me over a week to clean them. It was also within walking distance of shops and hospitals and of course pubs and clubs.

It was from here that we locked up the house and headed off around Australia.

We were towing a Suzuki Grand Vitara on the 'ReadyBrute' flat towing system which worked great, it was amazing how the car just followed the motorhome.

Leaving Cairns we headed to Victoria to visit some rellies first and then to South Australia to Port Macdonnell and all the way up the coast to Victor Harbour, what a rugged, yet beautiful coastline. The weather was very cold but we did not let that stop our discovery of some fantastic places.

Walleroo and up past Port Broughton then on to a few days at Port Pirie, up and through Port Augusta and around to Whyalla.

What a different town Whyalla was, it must have been great in its heyday with steel manufacturing.

It was here when our roof hatch above the shower blew off with the strong winds we encountered at the waterside caravan park. There was no one available to repair this in Whyalla and I had no means of getting on the roof. I asked at the caravan park for the loan of a ladder but due to Workplace Health and Safety, they said that they were not permitted to lend me a ladder.

We drove down to Port Lincoln where we found a caravan accessories that also did repairs.

They were really great, they had a replacement hatch in stock and fitted it within an hour. I also bought from them a folding ladder, which I never got to use.

We both absolutely loved Port Lincoln, except for the temperature, another amazing Australian City.

We then visited all the towns on the water until we got to Ceduna, what another great place and especially if you are an oyster eater, as I am.

I had tried oysters at every bay since Port Lincoln, starting from Coffin Bay and stopping at all eight other bays in between.

Arriving in Esperance after crossing the Nullabor, we then ventured in our little Suzuki up towards Cape Le

Grand, how beautiful is that place. The entrance to the National Park had a huge sign telling people who were travelling with pets to turn around.

Sadly entrance fees of $12 were required just to drive into the park to look at the beaches, if you want to camp there it's another $20 per person.

There are even cameras on the beach with EFTPOS machines, they record your number plate and if you don't pay you get a fine.

We found this at quite a few of the National Park attractions all the way up the coast.

Albany was just unbelievable, it is in my opinion the star of the West. Shoal Bay and King George Sound in Frenchman Bay, with the Whaling Station. I just loved everything about Albany.

I could go on and on, describing each City and Town all the way up the West Coast of Australia that we visited, but that would be another whole book.

I recommend the drive, I really do.

I was a bit disappointed in Broome, from what I had read and heard about it, but I suppose that I am spoilt by living in Cairns.

Going clockwise around Australia, everyone that we met on our trip, said it was the wrong way to go owing to headwinds which caused the vehicle to use more fuel. But we didn't care, we enjoyed every minute and it also gave us more information on what we were likely to encounter up ahead as we met with lots of travellers doing the trip anti-clockwise.

One such traveller told us that at Fitzroy Crossing, he had stopped for fuel and whilst inside paying for the fuel asked the woman there for a hamburger, the woman told him that by the time she had the hamburger cooked, the wheels from his car would be gone?

Many people warned us of Fitzroy Crossing and said that the only safe place to park up there for the night was the Fitzroy River Lodge, It's a great place with a nice tavern and bistro with a good atmosphere and good food, easy to find they said, just follow the signs.

We followed the signs to Fitzroy Crossing Inn by mistake and did not realize our mistake as we wheeled through the high gates into the big compound with its high walls and fences.

It wasn't until we went into the tavern for a drink that we started to have our doubts about the place. The bar was enclosed in steel mesh and there were signs which said 'If you drink here at day time, you can't drink here at night time' and 'If you leave here, you can't come back'.

We went into the Bistro to see if that was any better and to check out the menu for dinner.

We ended up just cooking something in the motorhome and drank our own stubbies, thinking that the fellow who was telling us how good it was must have been smoking something good.

The fellow at the reception when we had booked in for the night assured me that the gates to the Inn were closed and locked at ten o'clock at night and opened at six thirty in the morning.

I had to go to the loo at about two in the morning and I could see the gates were wide open.

It wasn't until we left the next morning that we drove past the Fitzroy River Lodge and then realised that we had stayed at the wrong spot.

Kununurra was another town we liked and spent nearly a week there then on to Katherine in the Northern Territory and then down to Mount Isa and Home.

In all we had been gone for almost five months, the whole trip was absolutely fantastic and we realised just how many places we just did not get time to visit and we have vowed to do it again, but next time differently.

It was at Monkey Mia in Western Australia, that we were talking to a couple who appeared to be about our age group. We had seen them at various locations, the first I think it was Ceduna when we first noticed them.

They were driving an older model Ford Ranger dual cab utility and I had asked what sort of a caravan were they towing, to which they had replied none. They had said that they were staying at either caravan parks in cabins or in motels.

A trip around Australia, they said, had been in their bucket list for some time and they had spent a considerable time talking to people who had completed the trip and how they had done it.

Consideration towards the cost of a caravan and tow vehicle including fuel costs had been calculated against the cost of travelling in a vehicle only and seeking accommodation on the way, the latter had proved to be a lesser cost by over fifty percent which had allowed them to do and see much more than the people towing caravans. So, that is how we will be doing our next trip around Australia. Looking forward to it!

Bundaberg

I was happy to get back to Bundaberg after nearly five months of travelling, Joy would have gone on travelling forever.

Part of the reason for selecting the home in Millbank was because it had two street entries.

It had its address entry in Voss Court and also another double gate entry in Isambert Lane.

We like the idea of a separate rear entry for the motorhome and safe storage in the locked rear yard.

When we first arrived at Millbank, the rear yard was all grass and the double gates were only one point five metres each, three metres total, which made it a bit too tight to get the motorhome through. We had plans to change this but for the interim, we kept the motorhome on the front driveway.

We were expecting a container that was carrying our furniture to arrive on the Monday, about a week after we had started to live there.

The people directly to the left of our rear gates would park their car directly in front of the double gates, On the day of the container's expected arrival, I saw that a person from that house at the rear gates was out in the garden and I introduced myself to her and said that we had a container arriving at these rear gates at some time this afternoon, and politely asked if She could move her car.

Her answer was, that they should be home all day and when the container arrived she would move her car.

Just as I was wondering how to put it to her that, her days of parking her car in front of these gates were over, a voice boomed from inside the open garage door of the house,

'And don't make it a fucken habit'

'I beg your pardon', I said as an athletic looking mature male stepped in to view from the garage.

'You heard me' he said very gruffly, 'That's not a gazetted driveway and those gates should not even be there, it's not your driveway and you can't park there'.

I was somewhat shocked, firstly the aggressive attitude of what was to be a new neighbour and secondly, the home we bought was advertised as 'two street access'.

I did not say a word to this person and went inside our house whilst rapidly thinking.

I explained to Joy what had just transpired out at the back gate and said that I am going to the council chambers to see if the home has gazetted dual access or not. If it did not have dual access we would be taking legal action against the real estate agent that we bought the property through, and that our solicitor, who had done the conveyancing, would be paying for the legal challenge.

The council completed a check while we waited and assured us that all was well, that we had dual access to our home and that it was illegal for anyone to park in front of the gates in Isambert Lane to our home, the council representative said that we should put signs on the gates and that he would organise yellow lines to be painted at the entrance to the gates.

The new, aggressive, neighbour seemed to have disagreed with the council's advice with the gate signs and the yellow painted lines as he still insisted on parking there.

I had called the council on a few occasions and finally, the council's controlled parking director, who was also a police officer, paid a visit to our 'Mr T' and told him that if he parked there he would be booked by either the police or by the council's parking officers. He stopped parking there.

We went ahead and extended the gates and entrance to four point eight metres wide and concreted the whole of the rear area, it proved to be an ideal area to park the motorhome.

It turned out that 'Mr T' was renting the house at the rear gates and a little down the track, the owner wanted to sell the property with a Tennant in place, but 'Mr T' refused any prospective buyer from entering the home and ended up packing up and leaving. That end of Isambert now became quite peaceful. The people opposite 'Mr T' also seemed to enjoy the new environment.

As fate would have it, it turned out that my former 'brother-in-law' was living near Bundaberg at the coastal town of Bargara.

Mick, was the husband of one of my former wife's sisters. It was Mick that had got me a job driving concrete trucks with him back in Canberra and we really got on well back then.

It was my former wife's sister who had found a new boyfriend, who just happened to be one of Mick's workmates? and had given Mick, the flick, pardon the pun, and he lived alone following the divorce, in a one bedroom unit at Oakes Estate, near Canberra, until he had retired at pension age and had moved to a warmer climate in Queensland.

Mick had been around to our place on occasions and we had gone out for meals at the Bargara Tavern with Mick from time to time.

He had shown us his great setup for getting to and from the tavern. The tavern was on the boundary of the retirement village where Mick lived and was separated by a high fence. Mick had somehow gotten hold of a key for the gate at the fence, and he would drive his car from his unit in the complex to the boundary next to the tavern, use his key and walk across the car park to the tavern. Perfect.

Sadly Mick passed away without my knowledge, however, one of my sons, who was friends with Mick's son, had contacted me and told me about his passing and I was able to contact Mick's daughter, Rebecca, who advised me that her mother was organising Mick's celebration of life at Mick's favourite drinking spot, the Bargara Tavern and she invited me to attend if I wanted to do so.

Of course, I wanted to attend! me and Mick went back a long way, like fifty three years. We were somewhat special really, we had been brothers-in-law, workmates and the best of mates, *no* I would not miss it.

There was no funeral, just a private burial and then this little send off.

There weren't many people there, his former wife, Lyn, his son and his daughter, who seemed quite pleased that I had attended their father's celebration of life, and a few of their friends. There was also one of his former wife's sisters, Jennifer, who was of course a sister to my former wife. When Jennifer saw me she screamed that I should not talk to her and to get away from her. She did this so loudly as to bring attention to her and in turn towards me that I felt so embarrassed and I felt that I should leave, which I did, much to the dismay of Mick's son and daughter. Mick was *my* mate. What a fucking bitch!

It was a beautiful home and as much as we enjoyed it, we came to realize that it was just too big, some of the kids only came to visit just once.

We agreed that, the house was too big and Bundaberg was too cold!

We decided to return to Cairns and put the mansion on the market.

We were looking out for a three bedroom unit on the Esplanade in the city, but there was none, other than penthouses at around two million dollars. Just a tad out of our budget.

We imagined that once our house was on the market that we would still have plenty of time to look around for a suitable unit in Cairns.

Well we were wrong, the house was sold within two weeks, or I should say the house was under contract within two weeks.

We had chosen the same agent that we had bought the home through as the selling agent. Although we were of the opinion that he was a sleaze bag, he seemed to move homes quite well around the area.

The agent had introduced a buyer and came to us with a contract that appeared to be acceptable with basically only two conditions.

The first condition was the usual pest and building inspection and the second was that the sale was subject to the buyer selling his property and it becoming unconditional.

We signed the contract and forwarded a copy to our solicitors for their perusal for conveyancing.

It was about two weeks into the sale when the clerk from our solicitor contacted me with the information that the buyer was happy to forgo the building and pest inspection in lieu of a roof plumber's inspection, our house had a flat roof with a box guttering system. She also advised that our contract would not become unconditional until the buyer's house sale became settled on the same day that our house was planned for settlement. I suggested to her that that could not be correct, surely the solicitor would have discovered that in the contract. The clerk remained adamant that was the case and said that the solicitor had not been aware of this instance and that she had since left the company.

I spoke to the principal of the law firm, whom I had met previously at a social occasion and he apologised but assured me that it should go through all right and that I probably had nothing to worry about.

Nothing to worry about! What it meant, was that the day our contract with the buyer became unconditional, was also the day that we had to settle with the buyer and hand over the home.

This left us in a predicament, that our furniture would be removed from the house and be in transit prior to settlement. If the buyer's home did not settle, then the buyer could pull from the sale of our house. What a fucking mess thanks to this solicitor who had now left her employment with the company that we had engaged for the settlement of our property.

There was little, or nothing that we could do, just hope it all went through.

The day of settlement for the buyer's home had arrived and we were loading the removalist's container with our gear. The buyers had purchased our furniture.

The buyer had also asked if they could store some of their items in the back of our property before settlement, which we had reluctantly agreed to.

It was during this time as the buyer was placing items into our backyard that he received a call from his solicitor advising him that his property would not settle on that day and that his buyer had sought a seven day extension on settlement.

This could not have been a worse situation for us, the buyer apologised but assured us that it would all go through, no worries. We had, already, had been assured that it would all go through, *'today'* with no worries and it *'had not*!

The buyer asked if he could have a key to the house in anticipation of the new settlement date of next week. We refused.

We felt that we had been conned by the real estate agent who had made such a deal with the buyers of our property, that if for some reason, the sale of their home did not go through, then they had no commitment to buy our home and would retain their deposit. The 'dumb' solicitor engaged with conveyancing our property did not see this written within the contract.

The worst that could happen to us was the huge waste of time, effort and money involved in packing, organising and paying for a removalist.

It would mean starting all over again selling the house.

We decided that we would go ahead with our move to Cairns and see what transpired with the seven day extension from the buyer of the people buying our home, confused?

The settlement did go through at the conclusion of the extension period and we were very relieved that we did not have to go through reselling the house.

The buyer of our home in this instance was, as he had told me, a very sick man.

He died just a year after moving into the home.

Back to Paradise

We both just love Cairns, while we were living in Bundaberg, four years in Bundaberg, we had visited the kids in Ravenshoe on occasions and it always included a stop in Cairns, it brought about a touch of homesickness.

The last time we visited Cairns was in the COVID-19 years between 2020 and 2021.

We could not believe the city was so quiet, so many places were closed and such few people were around.

Just for the experience, we travelled by train from Bundaberg to Cairns. The train left Bundaberg at six thirty in the evening and arrived in Cairns the next afternoon at two thirty, just on a twenty hour rail journey. But from memory, we were about two hours late for some reason or other. I do, however, remember feeling quite shattered as I arrived in Cairns.

I also remember the, what seemed like instant heat, it was just beautiful. But I was certainly *not* looking forward to the return trip to Bundaberg.

All subsequent trips from Bundaberg were by car.

Well here we were back in Cairns, our car was packed with the belongings that we thought we might need until we found a unit to move into. Our other belongings were packed into a container and would shortly be arriving in Cairns and would go into storage.

We had found a budget hotel/motel as we had no idea just how long it would be until we found a suitable unit and were unable to afford anything with luxury at around four hundred dollars a night.

I had assumed that there would be ample units in suitable or satisfactory locations to choose from.

Wrong,.. there seemed to be a shortage of units that would meet our criteria of;

Three bedrooms.

Two bathrooms.

On the Esplanade with either ground floor location, or elevator for upper level.

Watching 'realestate.com' closely every day, we would call the respective agent for any that we found that sounded a possibility, only to be told that they were under contract.

Even though we were, sort of, homeless, we were enjoying being back in Cairns and kept on looking and looking. We decided that we may have to change our criteria slightly from three bedrooms to two bedrooms as three bedrooms seemed to be a bit like 'rocking horse shit' around the city area.

After over three weeks of searching, Joy came across a really nice, two bedroom, two bathroom apartment on the Esplanade within our budget. It was on an upper level but had two elevators servicing the floors.

The unit was within a resort that had two swimming pools and a full gymnasium.

We fell in love with it at first sight and signed a contract for the purchase of the unit with a settlement of thirty days.

The day we signed the contract we went to the RSL club for a celebration drink and I won ten thousand dollars on the pokies, a good omen?

The thirty days until the settlement seemed to take forever but we had a great time selecting new furniture and televisions while waiting for the day to finally arrive.

As as it is often said: *'The rest is History'*

The End, *maybe!*

Have you read the preluding book to this?
Max Barrington has also written;
'The First Ten Years in Australia, by a Ten Year Old, Ten Pound Pom'.
It is the story of Peter Harris's journey from England in 1959 at the age of ten, with his parents and siblings.
This book is available in Paperback, eBook and also Audio Book.

Fifty Five More Years

Max Barrington

www.ingramcontent.com/pod-product-compliance
Lightning Source LLC
Chambersburg PA
CBHW072049290426
44110CB00014B/1609